Accounting Comes Alive:
The Color Accounting Parable

Mark Robilliard & Peter Frampton

TITLE
Accounting Comes Alive: The Color Accounting Parable

ISBN: 978-1-4507-6960-0

AUTHORS
Mark Robilliard
Peter Frampton

DESIGNER
Chang Won Chang

EDITORS
Mark Morrow
John Gorman

PRODUCER
Jenny Geier

ACCOUNTING
comes
ALIVE

The Color Accounting Parable

Mark Robilliard & Peter Frampton

WELCOME

Accounting is all around us. Many of us know that we should understand it because it is the language of personal and business finance. Whether you are buying a house, leasing a car, managing a store, starting a business, or paying a credit card… accounting is at work. Understanding the accounting principles that surround us will empower you. Being accounting-literate will enable you to see more clearly, ask better questions, and make better decisions.

For hundreds of years accounting has been hard to grasp. For example, accounting involves a duality (there are two effects when a single transaction happens), and accounting jargon is highly ambiguous (single words have many meanings). For these and other reasons people often talk at cross-purposes when learning or discussing accounting and financial matters.

At last, thanks to the advent of the color printer and the availability of graphical design programs, accounting can be presented visually. It's now easy to see double effects and to reveal ambiguous terminology.

Accounting Comes Alive: The Color Accounting Parable is an easy way for you to begin mastering the concepts of accounting, in a fun and enchanting way. The simplicity of the story about a grandfather teaching his grandson accounting and business belies the power of the learning.

HOW TO USE THE BOOK:

The Color Accounting Parable is an easy and engaging read. But to get the most benefit out of the story you still need to focus and get involved in the conversation. We suggest you read the story slowly and work through each diagram; they are the key to your understanding. The diagrams complement the text and build upon one another.

The three or four hours you will take to thoroughly work through the Parable could very well be the difference between passing and failing your exam, managing or mismanaging your business finances, or powerfully engaging your accountant instead of avoiding her.

Have fun, take it slowly, and set yourself free.

With best wishes,

Mark Robilliard and Peter Frampton
Founders, Accounting Comes Alive.

Accounting Comes Alive: *Business Comes Alive*

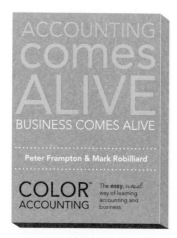

"A revolutionary book like no other."

"A game changer."

Debuting in early 2012, this seminal book is the flagship *Color Accounting* text that is set to change how accounting is learned. This textbook thoroughly explains the principles of accounting using the visual and easy-to-follow *Color Accounting Framework*. Because accounting concepts are simple when presented graphically, even so-called advanced topics are simplified in *Accounting Comes Alive: Business Comes Alive*.

Topics include balances sheets, income statements, cash flow statements, accounting principles, accrual vs cash accounting, ledgers, journals, ratios, financial analysis, surefire ways to increase the owner's return from a business, how to increase cash flow, and much more.

The book is a must have for accounting students, managers, small business owners, and professionals working with financial reports.

Available from AccountingSchool.com and select bookstores.

Accounting Comes Alive: Online Self-Study Solution

Arriving in late 2011, **Accounting Comes Alive: Online Self-Study Solution** is the breakthrough visual course that brings the power of *Color Accounting* to your web browser.

"A new freedom around balance sheets, income statements and business itself."

For over ten years, *Color Accounting Trainers* in Australia, Canada, South Africa, UK, USA, and elsewhere have been running one-day workshops for thousands of employees at leading banks, corporations, law firms, and small businesses. But not everyone likes learning in a classroom environment or has the opportunity to do so. The *Color Accounting Self-Study Solution* brilliantly captures the teaching techniques perfected in these live workshops to empower you and bring you unforgettable learning epiphanies. This visual and interactive program vividly brings to life the fundamental truths of accounting. You'll quickly understand how accounting works and be able to apply your learning long after you've finished clicking, drawing, listening, watching, and engaging.

Available at AccountingSchool.com.

TABLE OF CONTENTS

CHAPTER 1
THE TIMELY RETURN OF THE SENSEI

My name is Craig Mackey. Some months back, I decided to leave my well-paid corporate job and start a small business, but just the thought of taking this leap of faith dug up some serious reservations about my chosen path. So I guess it's not surprising that when I walked into my grandfather's small but successful business on the outskirts of Springfield, he knew exactly why I had come to see him.

"Pops, I think I'm finally ready," I said, skipping right past the enthusiastic greetings and hugs that were always part of our reunion ritual.

"Ah, yes," he said with an engaging smile, "I know. I've been waiting for you."

My grandfather Zach, affectionately known as Pops by the family, had for many years owned and run a small but successful general store and supermarket called Z-Mart in our neighborhood. Despite never receiving any formal business education Pops was successful in business. In fact, he had left school and got a job as soon as possible to earn money to help his parents. In his late twenties, he started Z-Mart in an empty building owned by one of our relatives. Now, in his sixties, he had started talking about succession planning and passing along what he knew about running a successful business.

We'd never talked seriously about business before, but it was clear I could learn plenty from him, despite my business degrees from two prestigious colleges hanging on my wall at home.

Like many with a business degree, I had done enough to pass the accounting classes and had even managed to complete an MBA online (with a lot of help on the accounting module). But the principles just didn't stick with me. And to be perfectly honest, I found the subject dull and boring.

As I considered my future as an entrepreneur, I knew my limited financial literacy was a potential disaster waiting to happen. Truthfully, I only had a basic understanding of finance and the proper recording and tracking of financial transactions, despite my years of being responsible for sales and marketing budgets. I knew (with some embarrassment) that I just didn't "get" balance sheets, income statements, ratios, and the basics of financing. So my grandfather was the obvious first stop on the road to financial enlightenment.

When I first approached Pops for help with my financial literacy, I expected him to pull out some financial statements from his files and explain the various elements of basic accounting to me. I thought that exercise, along with a little one-on-one coaching would be all I needed before moving on to the next signpost on my journey.

So I have to admit that I was surprised and a bit confused when he handed me a copy of an old movie about a kid learning karate from his mentor and suggested that I watch it. I had indeed seen the movie when it was first released and still recalled its basic message and story line. But what was behind Pops' request, done with that signature playful twinkle in his eyes?

"Can you tell me how you might apply the lessons of this movie to your own learning journey?" Pops queried.

"I have no idea," I replied with an appropriate look of confusion on my face.

"Sure you do," he continued. "Do you recall the frustration that the young boy felt when his Sensei made him do various chores over and over again such as cleaning his car, waxing the floor, and painting the fence when all he wanted to do was learn karate? What do you think was the point of the student doing all those strange exercises?"

"I don't know," I responded with a shrug.

"OK, then," Pops said. "I want you to go home and watch the movie, and then we'll talk more." And just like that, our first session was over.

As much as I loved Pops, I felt somewhat irritated by the assignment. "Why can't he just tell me what I need to know?" I thought. When I finally decided to humor him and watch the movie a few weeks after our meeting, the reason Pops gave me the assignment was perfectly clear and prompted a call to set up our next meeting.

I walked into Z-Mart a week later with an enthusiastic greeting of "Pops, I think I'm truly ready," and we settled into his small office at the back of his store. Pops didn't waste any time; once we both had a fresh cup of coffee in hand he immediately asked me about the movie.

"So, what is the message for us from the karate Sensei on this lovely Sunday afternoon?" he asked.

I quickly offered up two thoughts that clearly pleased him greatly: "The point of the seemingly pointless tasks that the Sensei asked the kid to do was to teach discipline and to program the most essential karate moves into his student's muscle memory."

"Exactly," he said.

"And that's the root cause of my own frustration and what has blocked me from successfully learning accounting in the past. I never established the discipline and mental muscle memory on which to base my accounting skills."

"Perfect," he said, thumping the table enthusiastically. "Now you are ready for me to teach you exactly what I've learned about accounting during all these years of running my own business."

I smiled, pleased to begin my learning journey with such a gentle and knowledgeable mentor.

CHAPTER 2
TWO-SIDEDNESS: OUR FIRST KEY PRINCIPLE

Later that afternoon, we walked the three blocks to Pops' house and settled into one of his familiar kitchen chairs before beginning the second lesson. My success earlier that day had bolstered my confidence, and now I felt absolutely prepared for the journey ahead.

Pops cleared his throat and started.

"It's time for you to learn the first principle of financial storytelling," he said. "Here, put your hand out." He placed an old, well-worn dollar coin into my hand. "I've had this coin for a long time, and it's been a big part of my success over the years. It's yours now."

I turned the coin over and over with my fingers, noticing how it felt. It was quite worn from many years of handling, and it felt warm and comfortable in my fingertips.

"What do you notice about this coin?" Pops questioned while looking at me over his reading glasses.

"Well," I started hesitantly, not immediately getting the point, "it is an old silver dollar coin."

"It is," Pops confirmed, "and it is much more than that." His challenge hung in the air, and I prayed I wasn't about to fail the first test.

"Relax," he teased before providing a clue, "notice the physical aspects of the coin." I turned the shiny coin over and over in my hand hoping the answer would come. Pops chuckled at my obvious discomfort and asked, "Can you see what your hands are telling you?"

Although still confused and unsure of the correct answer, I offered up my best observation. "Well I suppose it has two different sides," I said hopefully.

"It does," he beamed. "In fact, this coin has much more power than you realize because it embodies the first principle of financial storytelling: two-sidedness."

"I see," I said, still unconvinced.

"Watch this," he said patiently as he raised the coin to my eye level and held it up vertically with the edge toward me. "Do you see the edge of the coin up before you?" I nodded. He slowly turned the coin sideways so I could see each side in turn, "And do you see the two distinct sides?"

"I do see that," I said, before adding, "but everyone knows that old saying about two sides of the coin."

"Ah, maybe they do, but how many realize that this is the very basis of financial storytelling?"

Explaining the Two Perspectives

Pops continued, "Every financial story has two sides, two perspectives, and both are required to fully understand the complete financial story."

"Hmm," I pondered aloud.

"Let me show you," he said with the excitement of someone about to reveal a great secret. He reached dramatically into the drawer behind him and took out a leather-bound notebook with my name written in gold letters on the front. Printed underneath my name was the title "Financial Storyteller Extraordinaire". Then he took out a new packet of colored pens and markers, cracked open the notebook, and on the first page carefully drew the following diagram.

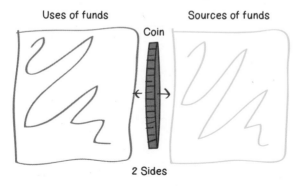

"OK," he said, "we just learned that your silver dollar coin has two equal sides. This is important information because this concept of "two-sidedness" or "duality" is the basis for understanding the entire financial story of any business, not just one aspect of it. The great news is that the financial storyboard I just drew here is the same one used by every business, large or small, around the world – the language of business and finance is truly global."

"It doesn't look like any business model I've seen before," I said.

"You will recognize and understand it soon enough," he assured me calmly before proceeding. "Have patience. On one side of the storyboard, we tell the story of the sources of a business enterprise's money. And on the other side, we tell the story of the uses of the enterprise's money. It's the same money, only a different perspective is applied to each side."

Pops picked up two markers from the table, one green and one yellow. "And we'll use these two colors of green and yellow as a convenient reminder of these two perspectives. And to make it real, let's use Z-Mart as an example and build our model from the ground up. But first, let's have a cup of tea."

Although I was anxious to learn more, I agreed that the interruption was a good idea and helped Pops set out the cups and prepare the tea. Then, with his favorite lapsang souchong brew steaming on the table he continued the lesson....

Starting Up a Business

"Imagine you are about to set up a corner store, like a Z-Mart. What things would you need to get started?" As I thought about my answer, he turned the notepad to a crisp new page, and with a pen in hand he waited for me to respond.

I visualized being inside Z-Mart and began my answer. "Well, you would need products to sell, some shelves and display bins, a display refrigerator, a freezer, a counter, a cash register, some scales, some baskets for the customers to shop with, some signs … stuff like that? Oh, and cash"

"Exactly," he beamed. "So, let's make a list." He drew a box, labeled it and filled it in with the things I had mentioned.

Things we need to start operating:

Products to sell
Shelving
Display Bins
Display refrigerator
Freezer
Counter
Cash Register
Scales
Shopping Baskets
Signs
Cash

Sources of funds
to get the
things we need
$$$

I piped up triumphantly, "Those things are all assets!"

"They are indeed," he confirmed. "Assets are a valuable component of every financial story. Soon we will work on the definition of the word assets so we can be very clear about what it does and does not mean. The language must be right before the financial story can make sense."

He pointed at the box and the list with his marker and commented that our business would actually need more assets than those we had listed, but this was a good start. Then he continued: "So, how do we get all the assets that our business needs to operate?"

"We need to buy them," I responded.

"Yes, and where will the money come from?" he queried.

I sipped my tea while contemplating his question. "You might have saved some money," I ventured.

"Indeed I did have a little bit of money put away when I started my business, but it wasn't enough to get all the things the business needed," he confirmed. "So I had to find the additional money somewhere else."

"And did you borrow it from a bank or a lender, perhaps?" I suggested.

"Yes, that's exactly what I did," he replied. "I contributed some money to the business from my savings and inheritance, and the rest of the start-up money came from a bank loan. Our business used all that money to fill up its bank account and later buy the other assets it uses to generate income. It doesn't matter if an asset is cash or an asset bought with cash, what defines an asset is value. Basically, if it has value, it's an asset."

"Now, before we get too excited," he continued, "we have two different funding sources in our financial story. The first is the loan made to the business, and the second is the owner's contribution to the business. In a traditional business story, the business owner's funding is separated from the other sources of funds." Pops moved my leather notebook closer to him and drew another storyboard. This time, the Z-Mart Financial Storyboard included a yellow dividing line in the sources of funds box. He labeled the top section 'Funding from others' and the bottom section 'Owner's contribution'.

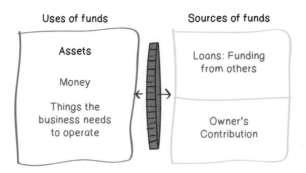

Uses of funds		Sources of funds
Assets Money Things the business needs to operate	←→	Loans: Funding from others Owner's Contribution

I got it immediately and excitedly chimed in, "That makes perfect sense! Of course, the owner wants to focus on their own part of the financial story."

Pops smiled broadly. "Indeed!" he said, "You have identified the second principle of financial storytelling: grouping. Let's freshen up our tea."

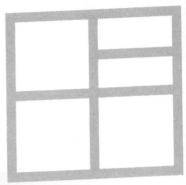

CHAPTER 3
GROUPING: OUR SECOND KEY PRINCIPLE

While I prepared our tea break, Pops used my activity as the basis for another lesson. "Craig, while you're over there, open the silverware drawer and tell me what you notice about the contents," he said.

I opened the drawer and leaned over to examine what seemed to be a fairly unremarkable arrangement of silverware.

"What story do the contents of the drawer tell you?" he asked.

"I see knives, forks, spoons," I answered.

"Good, but look beyond the obvious and notice something about the way the drawer is organized," Pops coached.

"The contents of the drawer are all sorted into types of silverware – the spoons are together, the forks, the knives – everything has its place"

"Exactly," Pops confirmed before continuing. "But why bother with the organization? Wouldn't it be quicker and less fuss to jumble everything in together rather than keeping them all sorted and neat?"

I thought for a moment and replied. "Well, the process of putting the silverware away would be quicker without organization. You could just throw it in, but the next time you needed a fork you would have to dig around to find it." Encouraged by his nodding, I went on. "And I suppose if you had guests over, you wouldn't immediately know if you had enough of each piece of silverware without unloading the whole drawer, sorting, and counting."

"Spot on!" Pops said. "And that's exactly why we have these separate areas in our financial storyboard – each has a piece of the story to tell. Businesses, large and small, process hundreds of transactions or more each day, and without a way to organize and track the transactions, a business would not know their financial position or be able to track their performance. Accounting, like my silverware drawer, is simply a way to organize information to tell a meaningful story and make better informed business decisions."

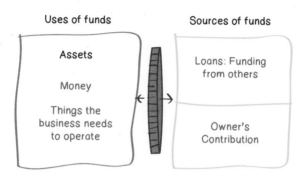

Uses of funds	Sources of funds
Assets Money Things the business needs to operate	Loans: Funding from others Owner's Contribution

Accounting had always seemed like a lot of jargon and hocus-pocus to me, but now it began making sense.

"We haven't named the two yellow sections of our storyboard, but I can tell you, without question, that the financial story of every business includes all three sections I am describing," Pops said emphasizing his point while tapping the drawing with his marker. Then he looked up and brightened his tone.

"Hey, I baked some muffins last night," he said, sliding back his chair. "Would you like something to eat?"

I nodded.

"Great, and then we'll continue our lesson," Pops got up and headed for a steel bin on the counter and popped open the container.

CHAPTER 4
Z-MART'S FINANCIAL STORY COMES ALIVE

With a muffin in hand, Pops continued the lesson.

"Let's make Z-Mart's financial story come alive by adding some transactions." Pops said, drawing the now familiar diagram into my notebook. "So let's say we borrowed $30,000 from a lender to start our business and we used that money to open a business bank account."

4.1   Z-Mart before loan funds received

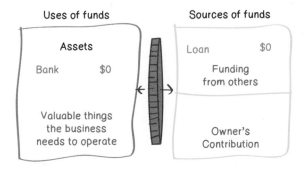

"Now think about the initial impact of that start-up loan on Z-Mart," he said. "Think about the real activity of the business sourcing that money because that's what we will represent on our storyboard."

"OK," I began hesitantly, "before we got the loan, nothing had happened in our story. We had a clean slate just like your diagram here." Encouraged by his nodding I continued, "When Z-Mart accepted the loan from the lender, the business suddenly owned $30,000 of real money which was banked in the business account. So the Z-Mart Bank account needs to be increased from $0 to $30,000."

"Excellent," he enthused. "You've told me what Z-Mart did with the physical cash, but you also need to describe the source of that money – the other side of the coin, if you will, on our storyboard," he said, eyes twinkling.

"Got it," I responded with excitement. "At the same moment as Z-Mart got the money from the lender, Z-Mart created a corresponding 'IOU' to the lender for the same amount of $30,000. The source of the $30,000 was a loan, and the money was used to fill up the bank account. So the loan account shown in the financial storyboard also needs to be increased from $0 to $30,000 because Z-Mart now owes $30,000 to this lender. Both sides of our storyboard are now in balance." I used my marker to adjust the financial storyboard to reflect my conclusion.

4.2   Z-Mart showing loan

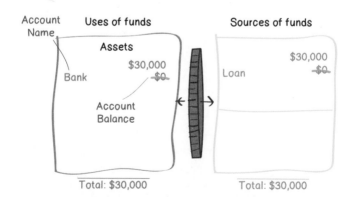

Pops smiled, "Right! The loan transaction has two effects on the storyboard. In fact, every transaction has two effects, although they don't have to be on different sides like this one. And by the way, because we are focused on language, trans-action is literally defined as actions that impact across – in this case, across the whole story. Each time Z-Mart has a transaction, there are two equal and opposite effects somewhere on our storyboard that will keep us true to our principle of two-sidedness. You will soon have an even better understanding of the 'equal and opposite' concept, but before moving on I want to add two more terms to our storyboard." Pops then used his marker to write out the words 'account name' and 'account balance' on the asset side of the storyboard and then drew lines to show 'account balance' was $30,000 and that 'account name' was bank.

In my notebook, he drew a pair of glasses and looking front on I could see one green lens and one yellow lens. Although confused initially, I decided to withhold judgment on the meaning of the glasses and wait for Pops to complete his drawing.

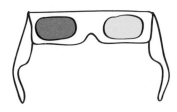

Unfortunately, my face was not as adept at hiding confusion. Pops noted my furrowed brow and assured me that the "unusual glasses" would play an important role in my education. Then he continued on with his instruction.

"Our duality principle is a bit like wearing these glasses: every financial transaction causes a green effect AND a yellow effect somewhere on the storyboard – sometimes both on the same side of the storyboard and sometimes on opposite sides, as we have seen."

"So what you are describing, in a creative way, is the concept of 'double-entry accounting', right?" Pops nodded and smiled at my observation.

"You know, I've heard this term used for years and it was never clear to me exactly what the term meant or how it was applied in a real business setting."

Laughing aloud at my confession, he nodded and said: "Yes, it's as simple as that. Like many of the business concepts everyone uses, double-entry accounting is shrouded in mystery and is just part of a universe of jargon. Double-entry is simply a different way of expressing the two effects of any business transaction; a green effect and a yellow effect is recorded every single time. And don't forget, this is also part of our duality principle: the storyboard always has two sides, and each transaction causes two effects somewhere on the storyboard"

I nodded my head to indicate I was starting to understand the concept.

"Perfect," Pops said. "As I mentioned earlier, I often refer to the overall combination of the two-effects and the two-storyboard sides as the 'accounting duality'. The term accounting duality captures both the double-ness of the effects and the double-ness of the sides. It's the overall double-ness. To me, understanding the concept of duality is key to understanding any financial story."

Pops took up his markers again and recorded the following transaction into my notebook. It reminded me of a diary entry.

Using Pops' Green and Yellow Glasses

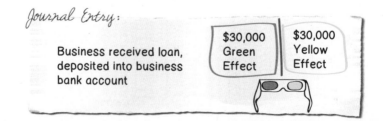

Journal Entry:

Business received loan, deposited into business bank account

$30,000 Green Effect

$30,000 Yellow Effect

Now, look at what I've drawn here and imagine that you are wearing your green and yellow glasses," he said, "and if you are ready I'll demonstrate a system that will track the green and yellow effects of any transaction on Z-Mart's storyboard."

"Lead on, wise one," I teased. Pops smiled and continued.

"This is the traditional way accountants set out a transaction that is ready to be recorded onto the financial storyboard. Accountants call the storyboard a general ledger and Z-Mart's initial loan transaction would be represented in this **journal entry** form. However, you have the advantage of your special glasses that allows you to see both the green $30,000 effect and the yellow $30,000 effect. In order to keep Z-Mart's financial storyboard in balance, we need to track both the green and yellow effects on the storyboard."

"That's right," I said confidently. "The bank account balance increased from $0 to $30,000 and so did the loan account balance. One was a green increase and the other was a yellow increase.

"Exactly," he beamed. "Now let's look a bit closer at how the effects impact the storyboard. And to do that, we'll use what I call color logic, or *Color Accounting.*" Now I was confused – *Color Accounting*? What next? Pops smiled, sensing my discomfort. "Don't worry," he said, "I just invented that name. I promise you'll really enjoy this next bit of the journey if you'll just stay with me for a few more minutes." Then he asked me this question:

"Has Z-Mart's bank account increased or decreased as a result of this first transaction?"

I thought that there must be some trick because the answer seemed obvious, but decided to play along. "Increased?" I answered.

"That's it!" Pops said. "There's no trick! Yes, the business bank account, Z-Mart's 'green account' on the storyboard, increased from $0 to $30,000. In our color language, you might say that the account is now 'more green'. So if you look through your green and yellow glasses, which of our two color effects do you think will make our green bank account become even more green?" he asked earnestly.

I chuckled, thinking that this exercise was absurdly easy. "The green effect," I said confidently. Pops was now laughing as well. "Thank goodness for those glasses," he said. "Now, if you can compose yourself long enough to answer another question for me, what color effect do you think will make our yellow loan account increase from $0 to $30,000 so that it becomes 'more yellow'?"

"Clearly, it's the yellow effect," I said.

"You got it," he exclaimed. Pops immediately began updating our Z-Mart storyboard, circling both the green $30,000 and the yellow $30,000 and adding a note about account balance changes with connecting dotted lines. Finally, he used black lines to connect the green $30,000 and the yellow $30,000 in the general journal graphic he had drawn earlier to the corresponding green and yellow side of the Z-Mart storyboard. "As you can see," he said, "the colors provide us with a sort of mathematical code."

4.3 **Z-Mart** showing journal entry for loan

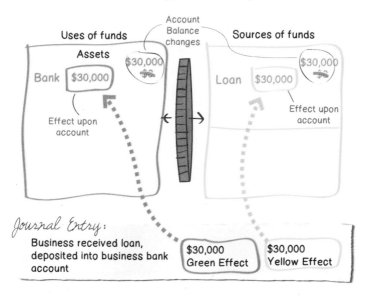

Yes, it all made sense now and seemed logical enough, but I still felt a baseline uncertainty that I couldn't explain. I posed a question I thought would help clarify my understanding, "So what happens if we spend some money out of the bank account? How would that be represented?" I queried.

"Great question," Pops said before launching into his answer, "If you think about the exercise we just completed, we represented an increase in Z-Mart's green bank account balance by using the green effect. If you put your green and yellow glasses back on, what color effect, green or yellow, do you think we would use to represent a decrease in Z-Mart's bank account balance?"

I imagined picking up the glasses and putting them on before answering. "It has to be the yellow effect. If the green effect represents an increase in the bank account balance then the yellow effect must reduce its balance, make it less green, so to speak. Since there are only two possible effects, it has to be the yellow effect."

"Spot on," Pops confirmed. "Our simple 'color-logic' rule supports the two-sidedness principle. It is how we represent the financial impact of transactions undertaken by the business." He paused before continuing, cautioning me to pay close attention to the next point.

"You must always have two effects on the storyboard: both effects may be increases, both may be decreases, or one an increase and one a decrease. And we'll sort this out later because it's not that important now. Let's take a break so that you can process all that you've learned so far, which is a lot."

With that, he closed out the lesson.

CHAPTER 5
THE TWO-SIDEDNESS PRINCIPLE RETURNS: JUST ADD COLOR

Pops left the kitchen for a few minutes, and when he returned, he suggested that I relax while he prepared for the next lesson. While I waited I tried to clear my mind for the upcoming challenge. Pops involved himself in an extensive drawing and labeling exercise in my notebook. When he was done, he looked up and complimented me on my understanding so far and posed a question I wasn't sure I could answer at first.

How Effects Impact Sides and Accounts

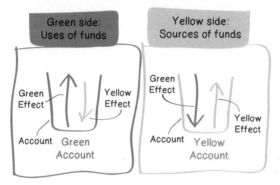

Every transaction has two effects: one green and one yellow. (The glasses remind us of this truth.)

The effects impact accounts. They do this according to the relationship between their color and the color of the accounts.

The two impacted accounts can be on the same side of the storyboard, or each on the opposite side - either way the sides of the storyboard will stay in balance.

THE UNIVERSAL RULE

↑ To increase an account balance, the color of the effect must be the SAME as the account color.

↓ To decrease an account balance, the color of the effect must be the OPPOSITE of the account color.

(Accounts get their color from the side they are on.)

"You've done quite well so far, and I can see you thinking deeply about what you're learning. So why don't you tell me everything you know about the principle of two-sidedness?"

"OK," I responded, trying to sound confident before launching right in to restate everything I could remember. "The financial story of a business has two sides, and both need to be told. Together the two sides tell the whole financial story of a business. One of those sides tells the story of the sources of funds for the business and the other side tells the story of the uses of those funds by the business. The sources side is yellow, and the uses side is green so we can tell them easily apart."

He nodded and urged me to continue.

"Because businesses have many transactions, it's important to record the financial impact of those transactions on the various accounts of the business. These accounts are located on either the green side or the yellow side of the storyboard depending on their type, like grouping silverware in a drawer. So far, we have created a green bank account and a yellow loan account on Z-Mart's storyboard.

"When a transaction impacts a business financially, it must be recorded against the accounts on the storyboard, which is our creative model of an accounting system or accounting general ledger. Each business transaction has both a green effect and a yellow effect of the same amount. You asked me to imagine a pair of glasses with one green lens and one yellow lens. The two effects, green and yellow, are part of the principle of two-sidedness and offset each other to keep the storyboard in balance. Having two effects is also known as double-entry accounting.

"A green account balance is increased by a green effect, and that means it becomes 'more green'. Similarly, a yellow account balance is increased, made 'more yellow', by a yellow effect. If the color of the effect is the same as the color of the account being affected, the impact of the effect is to increase the account balance.

"When we want to show a decrease in an account balance, we use the opposite color effect. For example, to represent a decrease in the green bank account, we use a yellow effect. It's like the bank account has become less green. Similarly, when we want to show that a yellow account has decreased, we use a green effect. The rule here is that if the color of the effect is the opposite of the color of the account being affected, the impact is to decrease the account balance.

"Finally, the green and yellow effects can go anywhere on the storyboard as needed to represent the two impacts of each transaction."

"Bravo!" Pops cheered. "You've picked this up very fast. Now, let's demonstrate two-sidedness in action with a few more examples from Z-Mart."

CHAPTER 6
FUNDS FROM THE OWNER

Pops turned over a fresh sheet in my notebook and quickly set up a new *Color Accounting* scenario for the next part of the lesson. With the framework completed in my notebook, he described a scenario to demonstrate the impact of a business owner's contribution of funds to the business.

"Now we need to account for the impact of the owner's contribution of funds to Z-Mart," Pops began. "Let's say that amount was $20,000. Can you tell me how this transaction might impact Z-Mart's financial story?"

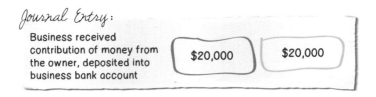

Journal Entry:

Business received contribution of money from the owner, deposited into business bank account

$20,000 $20,000

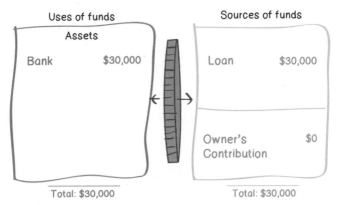

6.1
Z-Mart Balance Sheet
before recording owner's contribution

Uses of funds		Sources of funds	
Assets			
Bank	$30,000	Loan	$30,000
		Owner's Contribution	$0
Total: $30,000		Total: $30,000	

"Well, clearly Z-Mart's bank account will increase by $20,000, and because the bank account is a green account, we use the green effect to increase our bank account from $30,000 to $50,000. In other words, it becomes more green.

"The owner's contributions account is a yellow account because it is a source of funds. The increase in the bank account came from the owner's contribution so we use the yellow effect to increase the owner's contribution account, so the balance is now $20,000." I drew in the changes to Z-Mart's financial position on the financial storyboard in my notebook along with corresponding green and yellow arrows.

6.2   Z-Mart showing effects of owner's investment

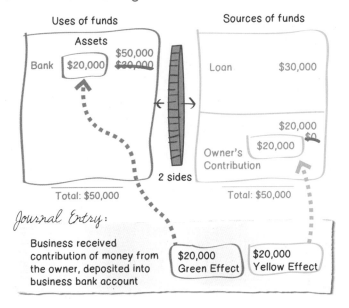

"That's perfect!" he said. "We now have an additional asset of $20,000 in the bank account, which came from the owner's contribution," Pops confirmed.

"In other words, say that our storyboard tells us that of the $50,000 in Z-Mart's bank account, $30,000 is owed to the lender and $20,000 is owed to you, the owner." I added.

"Nice observation," Pops said. "The two main money sources for the business, lenders and owners, do represent 'claims' against the assets of the business. Or to restate it, those individuals have a legal 'claim' against the assets of the business.

"As such, Z-Mart's loan account has first claim against the assets of the business ahead of the owners. In fact, the owner's claim usually ranks last in the event a business is closed down. It's unusual to talk about the business 'owing' the owner because the business is not required to pay the owner. But it's not entirely wrong to describe it like that.

"In the business world, the owner's investment in a business is always more at risk. The rewards come when a successful business pays dividends from the earned profits or the business grows or becomes more valuable and the owners are able to sell it for a profit."

"That's very interesting when you put it like that," I said, eager to demonstrate my understanding and enthusiasm to learn, "but I would have thought that investments would be shown in the assets section of Z-Mart's storyboard when you said that the owner invested their money into the business."

Pops grinned. "Good point, Craig!" he said. "And you have just brought us to the very next principle, the principle that accountants call 'entity theory'. I call it simply, 'whose story is it?'"

CHAPTER 7
WHOSE STORY IS IT? ENTITY THEORY:
OUR THIRD KEY PRINCIPAL

"When telling or interpreting a financial story, you need to be very clear about whose story it is. This may seem obvious, but forgetting the perspective of a story causes a lot of communication problems. Getting the perspective right helps get the language right," Pops said as he repositioned his chair closer to the kitchen table and quickly constructed three small storyboards in my notebook, labeling them Z-Mart storyboard, Bank of Tasmania, and Owner "X".

"Take Z-Mart for example," he continued, drawing a circle around the Z-Mart storyboard. "You might imagine a bubble around Z-Mart's storyboard. When telling the Z-Mart story, it must be from a perspective inside that bubble; not from the perspective of the lenders and not from the perspective of the owner. Lenders and owners each have separate financial stories, and both exist outside the entity bubble. For example, if the Bank of Tasmania was Z-Mart's source of money in our financial storyboard, that loan would be labeled as a use of money in the Bank of Tasmania's own financial storyboard." Pops added this additional information to the Bank of Tasmania and Z-Mart storyboards and drew a line connecting the two.

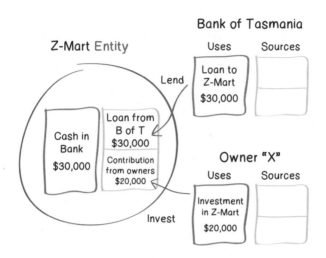

"It's the same for the money contributed by the owner," he continued, "from the owner's perspective, of course their investment in the Z-Mart business would be shown as a use of funds in the owner's story – an asset to be specific." He drew a line connecting the Owner "X" storyboard to the Z-Mart storyboard. "But from the perspective of the business, those same funds are a source of money. You see, it's all perspective and the language changes accordingly.

"Accountants call this the 'Entity Theory'," explained Pops. "The financial story is told from the perspective of the entity itself, rather than from the perspective of those who have provided the funds, whether they are the lenders or owners."

"That seems pretty obvious when you think about it," I replied. "Every transaction that Z-Mart has with another business must be recorded in the other business' accounting system and recorded from their perspective. For Z-Mart, the money we have deposited in our bank account is an asset to Z-Mart, but from this deposit-bank's point of view, it's like Z-Mart has loaned the money to them - they have borrowed it from Z-mart so they would show a liability in their storyboard."

"Ah-ha," Pops said slapping the table. "That's right, and it leads us to the next issue."

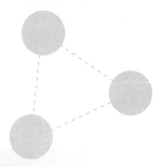

CHAPTER 8
THE THREE IMPORTANT PARTS OF EVERY FINANCIAL STORY

"So, let's review for a minute here," Pops said, picking up the green and yellow markers again.

"Z-Mart now has $50,000 in the business bank account. What do you think is the next item on our agenda?"

"That's easy," I responded. "Z-Mart needs to acquire those assets we listed earlier – display bins, freezers, cash registers, and so on – and start operating."

"Exactly," he confirmed, turning to a new page in my notebook and sketching out a new storyboard while continuing the lesson. "And to save some time, we'll combine the effects of all of those asset transactions together on this storyboard." Pops inserted three asset categories in the asset side of Z-Mart's storyboard – inventory, fixtures, and equipment – along with corresponding amounts for each that when added together totaled $26,000.

8.1 **Z-Mart** purchase of assets

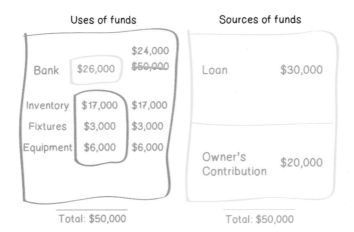

Uses of funds			Sources of funds	
		$24,000		
Bank	$26,000	~~$50,000~~	Loan	$30,000
Inventory	$17,000	$17,000		
Fixtures	$3,000	$3,000		
Equipment	$6,000	$6,000	Owner's Contribution	$20,000
Total: $50,000			Total: $50,000	

"Let me see if I can explain what happened here," I said, picking up an extra green marker from the table. "This is an example of the green and yellow effects impacting the same side of the storyboard. Z-Mart sort of swapped one asset, cash, for some other assets; inventory, fixtures, and equipment. The bank account has decreased by $26,000, and we've shown this by using a yellow effect, which has a reduction impact. We spent the $26,000 from the business bank account on other assets that the business needs in order to begin operating. We've shown this with three green effects that have an increase impact. Nothing needs to change on the sources of funds side because there was no effect on sources of funds to the business."

"That's right," Pops confirmed. "Remember, our financial storyboard is a model of Z-Mart's financial reality. It's describing a real situation. In the shop, there would now be real inventory ready to sell, real fixtures, and real equipment. The cash would be in the business account at the bank.

"The business owes money to the lender, and the owner has contributed some of their own cash to the business. And the standardized measuring tool for each account in the story? The dollar amounts indicated."

"Z-Mart's starting to look like a real business now," I added.

"Yes, indeed," Pops said with a smile before continuing. "But we have some more work to do and concepts to explore before we're ready to begin operation."

Pops pointed to the Z-Mart storyboard with his marker. "Let's look at our storyboard again. We have assets in our business, but what do you think accountants call the two yellow sections of our storyboard?"

"I know that the loan account section is where we show what the business owes – its debts," I answered.

"Exactly. Accountants call this section the liabilities. We'll sort out the definitions of all three sections shortly. What do you think accountants call the owner's contribution section?"

"I'm not sure," I responded. "But clearly this section is all about the owners and their claim on the assets."

"You're spot on," Pops said. "That is an excellent description. Accountants call this section of the financial story, equity." He smiled. "Well done. Every financial story has these same three fundamental sections: assets, liabilities, and equity."

"Wait a minute," I exclaimed, excited to make a connection familiar to my work. "Assets, liabilities, and equity are the three sections of a balance sheet!"

"You are correct" he confirmed, then turned to another page in my notebook and constructed two more storyboards. "Every balance sheet has these three sections. But instead of showing the story balanced horizontally, the modern balance sheet shows it vertically, like so..." And with this last point he drew a minus sign and an equal sign, then finished labeling the two storyboards.

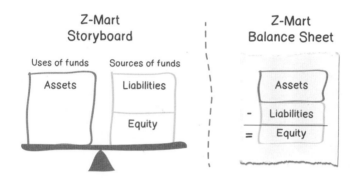

"You can see that the two storyboards are the same and that only the layout is different. Notice also that the underlying formula in the balance sheet that tells us quickly what the owners claim is worth, at least according to the books anyway."

"Yes, I do see that now. Funny, but I never really thought of equity in that way. It's actually the owner's share in the value of the assets, once the liabilities have been settled."

"You've done amazingly well today," Pops said as he closed my notebook and gathered the colored pens and markers. "Let's call it a day, all this excitement is tiring! Tomorrow we'll begin with important definitions."

I walked out into the evening air surprised how quickly the time had flown. For the first time I actually understood the financial story unfolding before me. We had covered a remarkable amount in a short time, and I was eager to learn more about business.

CHAPTER 9
GETTING CLEAR ON ASSETS, LIABILITIES, AND EQUITY

The lessons I learned from Pops brought new meaning to my work the next day. As I looked around, I noticed for the first time that I was surrounded by the assets of my firm and I mentally placed tables, chairs, computers, and file cabinets on the firm's balance sheet as assets and wondered if the assets were being funded by debt (liabilities) or by the owner's equity. By the time I pulled up a chair again at Pops' kitchen table in the late afternoon, pens and markers placed carefully beside a blank page in my leather notebook and a cup of tea steaming next to me, I could hardly contain my enthusiasm.

As I described my day and how I had applied the lesson of the previous day, Pops opened my notebook and sketched out a Z-Mart balance sheet as our starting point for the day.

9.1 **Z-Mart Balance Sheet**

Uses of funds		Sources of funds	
Assets		**Liabilities**	
Bank	$24,000	Loan	$30,000
Inventory	$17,000	Claims by others	
Fixtures	$3,000	**Equity**	
Equipment	$6,000	Owner's Contribution	$20,000
Money in use		Claims by the owner	
Total: $50,000		Total: $50,000	

"Our storyboard is evolving nicely," he began, "but before we go on we really do need to be sure we understand the exact meanings of the three key words: Assets, Liabilities, and Equity. I know these are commonly used words in business, but for the most part few understand their real meanings. Because assets are central to any business story, let's start there. How would you define assets in simple terms?"

"Assets are things of value that the business owns," I ventured.

"Yes, that is a good starting point," Pops agreed. "Assets are valuable, we can measure what they cost us, and they will bring benefits to our business as we use them in the future. Assets can be used directly or indirectly by the business to earn money. For example, when you sell inventory, it is being used directly in the money-making process. On the other hand, fixtures or equipment are used indirectly to make money.

"What about liabilities?" Pops queried.

"I would define Liabilities as being the amount the business owes – its debts. If you look on Z-Mart's balance sheet it is clear what the business owes right now, and we also know that Z-Mart has to meet these obligations sometime in the future."

"That's good enough," Pops said. "So, how will Z-Mart meet those debts in the future?"

"I expect that Z-Mart will use whatever money is in the bank account to meet those debts," I answered. "And the business will need to make sales sufficient to generate money to service those debts!"

"Good answer. That's by far the most common way for a business to meet its debt obligations, and in reality the business could use any of its assets as payment, so long as both parties agreed.

"Now, tell me about equity," Pops said taking a sip of his tea. "How would you define equity in simple terms?"

I thought about my answer for a moment before answering. "We've already talked a bit about equity and its relationship to the assets so I would define equity as being something like 'the owner's share', or 'our share' if we are the owners."

"That's pretty good," he said, "but tell me this – the owner's share of what?"

"Equity represents the owner's share of the assets once all of the liabilities have been met. The amount of equity is calculated as the leftover amount, or residual."

"Great answer, Craig – well done," Pops told me. "And to be sure, equity is not a physical part of the assets; it's a partial claim on the assets. Equity is never physical. Just like liabilities, equity is an intangible concept. It's a right or a claim – a legal concept, you might say. Equity describes rights to the assets. People often confuse equity with the associated asset itself, but it's a legal and financial concept. An accountant might call that concept the 'net assets' or even the 'book value of the business'. Let's get all this down in your notebook."

Pops picked up a black marker and added new labels to the Z-Mart balance sheet storyboard while I watched, fascinated by how quickly he worked.

9.2 Z-Mart Balance Sheet with definitions

Uses of funds

Assets	
Bank	$24,000
Inventory	$17,000
Fixtures	$3,000
Equipment	$6,000

Own.
Valuable things.
Nice to have.
Provide ongoing
benefits to business.

Total: $50,000

Sources of funds

Liabilities	
Loan	$30,000

Claims by others.
Owe. Debt.
Present obligation.
Future outflow of funds.

Equity	
Owner's Contribution	$20,000

Owner's share of
asset's value.
Residual. Remainder.
"Net assets".

Total: $50,000

"That's really helpful," I said. "I can see the value of Z-Mart's assets on one side, and on the flip side I can see who has got a claim on those assets – those to whom the business owes and also the owner's share of the assets. In fact, using the labels you provide, I might say that Assets equals Liabilities plus Equity."

Pops smiled. "That's clever of you! You've just explained Principle Four, the Accounting Equation."

CHAPTER 10
THE ACCOUNTING EQUATION:
OUR FOURTH KEY PRINCIPLE

My mind was whirling with all of these new concepts. Apparently I had just discovered the Accounting Equation. I had encountered the term in school but now its meaning was clear. While I worked at dredging up the faded memories of accounting classes taken many years ago, Pops turned to a new page in my notebook and created a new Z-Mart balance sheet to demonstrate the concept.

10.1 Z-Mart Accounting Equation

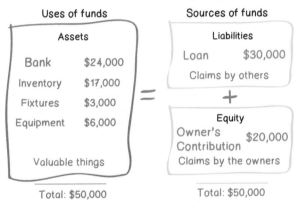

Uses of funds		Sources of funds	
Assets		**Liabilities**	
Bank	$24,000	Loan	$30,000
Inventory	$17,000	Claims by others	
Fixtures	$3,000	+	
Equipment	$6,000	**Equity**	
		Owner's Contribution	$20,000
Valuable things		Claims by the owners	
Total: $50,000		Total: $50,000	

While the initial drawing of the Z-Mart balance sheet was familiar, he added two new elements below the balance sheet. The first was the formula, A=L+E. Underneath the formula, he constructed a corresponding green box under the "A" and two yellow boxes under the "L" and "E." Inside the colored boxes he wrote Assets, Liabilities, and Equity and gave each a value taken directly from the Z-Mart balance sheet.

Next, he constructed the exact same set of green and yellow boxes again, but created a new formula, A-L=E. In this case, assets minus liabilities equals equity had a very different focus.

Two forms of the Accounting Equation

$$A = L + E$$

| Assets $50,000 | = | Liabilities $30,000 | + | Equity $20,000 |

$$A - L = E$$

| Assets $50,000 | − | Liabilities $30,000 | = | Equity $20,000 |

"Do you recognize these formulas?" Pops asked me. "I suspect you've seen them in some form during your time at business school." I admitted that I had, but now understood them. "Good, but I don't want to dwell on these formulas now as they are really just a restatement of our storyboard. First, we need to understand how a business makes a profit, and then we'll explore these concepts. I promise that once we do come back to study these formulas that you'll see how business and accounting will come alive. By the way, which one of these formulas do you think business owners use the most?" he asked.

"Clearly, the second formula," I answered. "It focuses on their share."

CHAPTER 11
THE FINAL TWO STORYTELLING PARTS ARE REVEALED

"OK Craig," Pops said, sliding his chair closer to mine. "It's time this business started earning some profits. Our assets are in place, and now we'll to put them to work. You've worked for a few businesses over the years, so tell me, what is profit, in simple terms?"

"That's an easy one," I began confidently. "Profit is the difference between income and expenses. We buy items to sell to our customers. We buy those items at a certain purchase price. We then add a margin to the purchase price to give us the sales price – which is the price that our customers pay."

"That's right," Pops said. "And how much margin do you add to the purchase price and why?"

"At our business, we add a standard 150% to the purchase price of all our products," I said. "With that margin, we are able to cover our expense of purchasing the item and the other expenses of running our business. Once we have sold enough products to cover all of the other expenses, then we start to earn an overall profit for the business."

"Good," Pops said enthusiastically. "Now, I'm wondering if you can put some of your artistic talent to work and draw what you just described as a model in your notebook."

Pops pulled out more markers just in case more colors were needed to tell my story. I decided to use the sale of a cookbook from Z-Mart as a vehicle to illustrate my points.

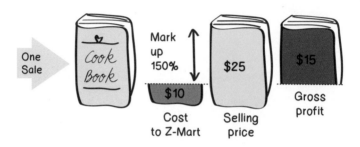

I began my illustration with a representation of a cookbook and gave the item a retail price of $25, a markup of 150%, and a cost to the business owner of $10, which left a gross profit of $15. I described each drawing and label to Pops as I created it, giving detailed explanations along the way.

"Now, the $15 gross profit on a single book doesn't contribute much toward covering our other expenses, but if we sell enough books we will eventually breakeven when we make enough to pay the other expenses of running the business. Once we reach the break-even point, every sale after that contributes directly to the earning of a net profit.

"At our company, we track the progress of the profit earned each month. We do this as a financial health indicator; both as a way to compare current performance with budget predictions and to compare our current performance with the previous year's performance."

He smiled and complimented me on my drawing ability and the information I had presented. "That's a very good illustration and explanation of profit. But where might you find this profit concept on a balance sheet?" Pops pulled my notebook closer and thumbed back a few pages until he found the last balance sheet storyboard we had done for Z-Mart. "So, where should the profit go on this balance sheet?"

11.1 Z-Mart Balance Sheet

Uses of funds		Sources of funds	
Assets		**Liabilities**	
Bank	$24,000	Loan	$30,000
Inventory	$17,000		
Fixtures	$3,000	**Equity**	
Equipment	$6,000	Owner's Contribution	$20,000
Total: $50,000		Total: $50,000	

I was a bit confused by this question. I had always looked for profits in the Profit-and-Loss Statement, also referred to as the Income Statement. How could the profits be in the balance sheet? I tried to sort it out by articulating what I knew.

"Profits are money, and money is an asset so I would expect profits to be shown in the assets," I said while looking out the window in a voice that was barely audible. But my musings must have been loud enough for Pops.

"You would think that and you would be partially correct," said Pops. "Profit is what we do that results in more assets, usually money. Money shows up in the business because of profit. So profit is connected to the assets, but it is not an asset itself."

"Here's another question for you," Pops said, leaning back in his chair. "Let's think about it from a different perspective. Is profit a source of money or a use of money to the business?"

"It's got to be a source of money," I answered. "It's money earned by the business from its customers, so it is the source of money coming in."

"Yes, it's the earning of the money," Pops confirmed while adding a follow-up question. "And where would you store any money that came in from earning a profit, at least initially?"

"In the business bank account," I answered. "The profit account shows us how much profit the business has earned, but the actual money earned is shown as an asset, in the bank account. This is that two-sidedness principle again!"

"You're quite right." Pops confirmed before posing another question. "You correctly stated that profits are a source of funds, but will their story be told in liabilities or equity?"

"That's an easy one," I said confidently. "Profits are not liabilities because we don't owe them to anyone – and we haven't increased our debts because of them. We did not make the bank manager richer! Profits are earned to ultimately benefit the owners of the business so the profit must belong in equity. They are part of the owner's funds."

"OK then," he continued. "So let's add a purple box to our balance sheet to signify where the profit account sits in equity." Pops drew a box around the yellow word Profits under the equity label on Z-Mart's balance sheet and posed yet another question.

11.2 Z-Mart Balance Sheet with profit account

Uses of funds		Sources of funds	
Assets		**Liabilities**	
Bank	$24,000	Loan	$30,000
Inventory	$17,000	Claims by others	
Fixtures	$3,000	**Equity**	
Equipment	$6,000	Owner's Contribution	$20,000
		Profits	
Money in use		Claims by the owners	
Total: $50,000		Total: $50,000	

"Now, an easy question: As the business earns profits, how will earning profits impact the size of its equity?"

"It will increase," I answered with authority. "As the profits are earned, the amount in the equity section in our storyboard increases, which makes the owners very happy. The amount in the asset section would grow as well because the proceeds of the profit show up in the bank account."

"Well done," Pops said, "now let's focus on the profit story some more."

"Yes please," I answered, "because I now understand why the profit lives in the equity section of the balance sheet. But I would love to understand more fully the concept of profit-and-loss statements. I get one each month at work, and I know they have to fit into this story somewhere!"

"Let me ask you this," Pops responded. "What story do your profit-and-loss statements tell you?"

"That's easy." I said. "The reports show the income we have earned for the month, less the expenses for that month, and this gives us a profit or loss figure for that month. The reports often have fiscal-year budget and year-to-date columns for comparison."

Pops picked up a black marker and turned to a fresh sheet in my notebook. As he notated the simple financial model, he explained the meaning. "We take the income earned by the business over the year, and then we deduct the expenses we incurred in earning that income. The difference will be a profit, or maybe a loss."

"So the profit-and-loss statement gives the detail of how the business got the profit," he said emphasizing the word profit. "It tells the story of how we made the profit. It shows the income less the expenses over some period of time and then gives a profit or loss figure."

$$\begin{array}{r} \text{Income} \\ - \ \text{Expenses} \\ \hline = \ \text{Profit (Loss)} \end{array}$$

"Exactly!" I confirmed.

"So watch this," he said mischievously. He added two new sections under the balance sheet, one labeled expenses and one labeled income with a profit and loss statement label above them. Then he tapped his pen twice on the yellow word 'Profits' in the equity section. "It's a bit like when you're using a computer and you double-click on a folder and a new window opens up underneath showing you two subfolders. The big purple box that I've just drawn is like the new window that appears, with two folders in it."

11.3 Z-Mart Storyboard with Profit & Loss Statement

Uses of funds		Sources of funds	
Assets		**Liabilities**	
Bank	$24,000	Loan	$30,000
Inventory	$17,000	Claims by others	
Fixtures	$3,000	**Equity**	
Equipment	$6,000	Owner's Contribution	$20,000
		Profits	
Money in use		Claims by the owners	
Total: $50,000		Total: $50,000	

Profit & Loss Statement

Expenses	Income

"So, what is our storyboard now telling us about Z-Mart?" he asked.

I thought for a moment before answering. "We have added a profit-and-loss storytelling section to our storyboard in order to explain the details of how we generated the profit number that currently sits in equity. The P&L is connected to the balance sheet!" I exclaimed.

"Yes, now go on, what else do you notice?"

"The income earned is a 'source of funds' to the business, and that's why it is on the yellow side of the storyboard. Income earned has the effect of increasing the profit," I emphasized unambiguously. "And expenses are 'uses of funds', and that's why they are on the green side of the storyboard. Expenses incurred have the effect of decreasing the profit."

"Great job," Pops said. "In fact, you are doing so well that I think you are ready to see the magic of profit and its impact on our storyboard."

"Bring it on," I said with a bit of swagger.

CHAPTER 12
GETTING CLEAR ON PROFIT: INCOME AND EXPENSES

Before continuing our lesson, Pops asked me to re-create my cookbook example on a fresh page of my notebook. While I set up the example again, he brewed some coffee to beat back my end of the day energy lows. When my example was complete, I held it up for him to see.

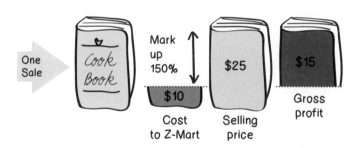

"Excellent," he said. "Let's initially identify where on the storyboard the book that we plan to sell is represented ."

"We'll review our previous work," Pops began as he brought my coffee to the table. "Take a look at the Z-Mart balance sheet we created earlier. The original cost of the book to Z-Mart has already been recorded on the storyboard when we bought the book. Can you find where it might be?"

I turned back to the Z-Mart balance sheet page and looked at the storyboard concluding that the book and other products we were holding for sale to our customers would be an asset. "The purchase price would be in the inventory account of $17,000," I answered.

12.1   Z-Mart Financial Storyboard

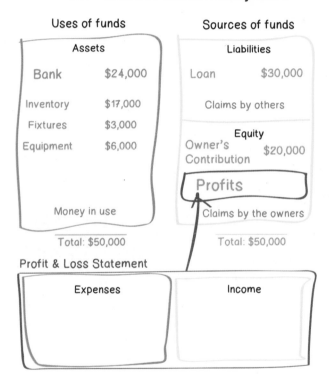

"That's right," Pops confirmed. "Just keep your notebook open to that page because we are going to do a lot more work with your cookbook example. So, let's assume that you've just sold one cookbook. We'll need to record the financial effects of the sale of the cookbook.

"To keep things simple, let's say it's a cash sale. The sale would look something like this." He drew three boxes in my notebook just like the journal entries created earlier, carefully filling in the appropriate information and amounts.

Journal Entry:

Cash sale of one cookbook $25 $25

"Where will the green and yellow effects go on our storyboard?" Pops asked me as he redrew a diagram at the bottom of the Z-Mart balance sheet using the green and yellow markers to construct two boxes (one green and the other yellow). He labeled one side "Green side: Uses of funds" and "Yellow side: Sources of funds" with the color-math arrows in each showing the increase-decrease rule for each side of the storyboard.

How Effects Impact Sides

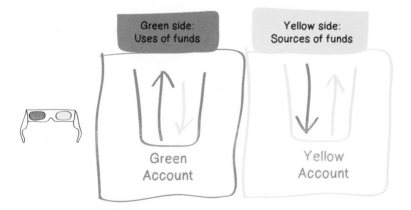

Green side: Uses of funds

Yellow side: Sources of funds

Green Account

Yellow Account

"Well I know the first part for sure," I began. "The cash we received from the customer would go into the business bank account and increase it from $24,000 to $24,025. According to our duality principle, the bank account is a green account and we want to show an increase in it. Therefore, we use the same color effect, the green effect".

"Bravo," he exclaimed. "That is absolutely correct. Now what about the yellow effect? What else was affected by this transaction?"

"This is the tricky part." I said. "My first thought is to say that we need to record the decrease in our inventory because one of our books has been sold."

"That makes some sense," he replied. "But you're getting ahead of the current lesson a bit by thinking of the cost of sale. We'll take up the expense associated with giving up the book in a moment, but first let's finish describing the actual sale event to the customer. Have you described the source of the $25 cash yet?" asked Pops, giving me a hint.

"Of course, I see now," I continued. "We haven't described the action of selling the book, which must be the yellow $25 effect."

He was smiling so I continued. "The sale of $25 is a source of funds to us – it's income we have earned. The sales account needs to be increased by $25 to reflect the selling of the cookbook. To increase the yellow sales account, we use the same color effect, the yellow effect." I grabbed the green and yellow pens and showed an increase in the business bank account in assets by $25 and correspondingly increased the sales account in income also by $25.

12.2 **Z-Mart** effects of sale of cook book

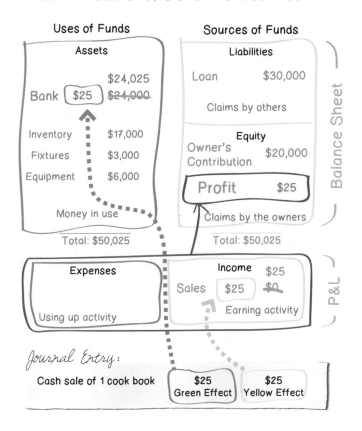

"Good," Pops said. "You know, one of the most common mistakes people make is to confuse the sale of inventory with the cash. Sales, also called revenue, is not cash. It's the work or activity that we do that brings in cash or other assets."

"This seems simple enough," I added. "Honestly, I thought this would be more complicated."

He smiled and replied, "It's like many things we think are complicated, once we break them down into bite-size pieces they are much easier to digest and understand. So, we're past the first hurdle of correctly recording a sale," Pops continued, "but we've only finished half the work we need to do on this sales transaction."

I looked at Pops with a confused expression, but soon recovered and offered a solution. "Well, we haven't recorded the fact that the cookbook is no longer part of our inventory. Our value of inventory has decreased because we've sold the book and we need to show that."

"That's exactly right," he confirmed. "It's called recognizing the cost of sale. For this selling event, one asset – our bank account – has increased because of the sale, but as a result another asset – our inventory – has decreased. We need to record the whole story of the sale – the sale and the corresponding cost of sale. So tell me, by what amount do we reduce inventory?" Pops queried.

"We need to reduce inventory by $25," I offered. But seeing the expression on Pops' face, I immediately reversed course. "Hang on, that can't be right. That's the sale price of the book, but it didn't cost the business $25 to buy the book." Then I realized my error. "The book originally cost us $10, and that's how much we recorded it in our inventory account in the balance sheet. So we need to reduce our inventory by $10, not $25!"

Pops listened to my self-instruction and inserted the amount in a journal entry form he had drawn in my notebook. Then he encouraged me to continue thinking through the transactions.

Journal Entry:

Sale of one cookbook - recording cost of sale	$10	$10

"OK, we know that the value of our inventory account has decreased by $10. According to our two-sidedness principle, to reflect a decrease you use the opposite color effect. The inventory account is green, and so to decrease it from $17,000, we need to use the yellow effect."

"But I have the green effect to deal with?" I continued. "I have already recorded the reduction of inventory by $10, so our assets have been reducec. What do I do with the green effect?"

Pops chimed in with a clarifying question. "On our storyboard, where do you think we might record activities that represent a loss of value of our assets?" Pops offered, "After all, most of them will lose value eventually, and we need to record the process of losing value somewhere."

As I looked at the storyboard, there could only be one place where this could occur, expenses. "But I always thought that expenses were just cash out in doing business," I said, thinking out loud.

"That is possible," Pops agreed, "but we need a more helpful working definition of expenses than that. Remember, the story of the business is all about value. If the item has financial value to the business going forward, then it is an asset. If the item doesn't have this value because the value has been used up/consumed/lost, then the consumption is an expense. Simply put, expenses are the loss of value to the business. It's the opposite of income, which is the generation of value to the business. Both income and expenses describe activities; income describes value generation activities and expenses describe value destruction/reduction activities." Pops paused to make another observation about financial misconceptions. "You know, many people think of expenses as 'cash out', but expenses are not cash out.

Cash may flow out of the business as a result of an expense, but the cash going out is not itself the expense. That's just spending – you could equally spend money to acquire an asset or pay off a liability. The cash outflow in this example is a consequence of the expense being incurred."

To illustrate his point Pops leaned over and grabbed a muffin. "In our bakery department, this pristine muffin constitutes an asset. And the eating of it, represents an expense," he exclaimed just before opening his mouth and theatrically taking a bite out of it.

12.3   Income and Expense definitions

Uses of funds		Sources of funds	
Assets		**Liabilities**	
Bank	$24,025	Loan	$30,000
Inventory	$17,000	Claims by others	
Fixtures	$3,000	**Equity**	
Equipment	$6,000	Owner's Contribution	$20,000
		Profits	$25
Money in use		Claims by the owners	
Total: $50,025		Total: $50,025	

Balance Sheet

Expenses	Income
Value sacrificing activity. Using up. Consumption. Devaluation. Depreciation. Destruction. Verb concept!	Value generating activity. Earned. Work performed. Sales. Revenue. Verb concept!

P&L

"OK, I get it now," I told Pops. "The $10 loss in value by handing over the sold book to the customer is an expense, so we need to increase expenses by $10. Expense accounts are green, so to increase a green account we use the same color effect, green!" I exclaimed proudly.

"You got it. The expense account would fit into the category of expenses called 'Cost of Sales', and we can think of it as 'Inventory Used Up' or 'Purchases' as it is often called."

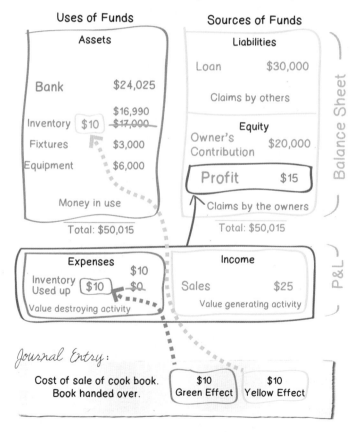

12.4 **Z-Mart** showing effects of loss of inventory (cost of sale)

Pops approved of my updated diagram. "Yes. If we stopped the clock right now, we can see that the P&L statement is showing a profit of $15 from this one sale. That is, sales of $25 minus inventory used up of $10. Now follow the $15 profit in the P&L statement up the purple arrow to where its net balance lives in equity – remember the 'double-click'! That $15 increase in profit is matched by a $15 increase in total assets; the bank account increased by $25 but inventory decreased by $10, giving a net increase in assets of $15, matching the increase in profit of $15 in equity."

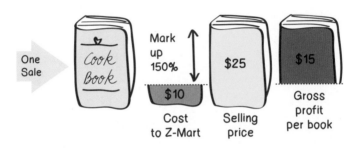

He smiled: "Before we get too comfortable, let's record one of those other expenses you were talking about earlier in your cookbook example." He flipped back to the page in my notebook where I had drawn the model. "Now we're going to talk about overhead expenses."

"Let's say that we just used a business check to pay the electricity bill for Z-Mart, and the bill was for $150. How would we record that expense?" Pops then drew another journal in my notebook, inserting the correct amounts in the green and yellow boxes.

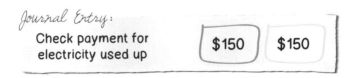

12.5 Z-Mart Storyboard

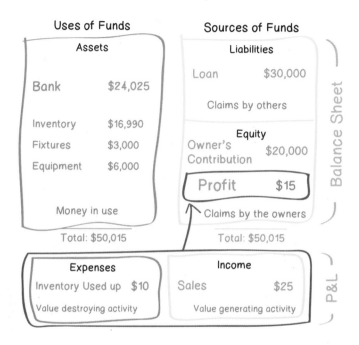

Uses of Funds

Assets

Bank	$24,025
Inventory	$16,990
Fixtures	$3,000
Equipment	$6,000

Money in use

Total: $50,015

Expenses

Inventory Used up $10

Value destroying activity

Sources of Funds

Liabilities

Loan $30,000

Claims by others

Equity

Owner's Contribution $20,000

Profit $15

Claims by the owners

Total: $50,015

Income

Sales $25

Value generating activity

Balance Sheet

P&L

"Well, we know that the bank account has decreased by the check amount of $150," I offered. "So that's easy. A decrease in the bank account, which is a green account, is represented by using the opposite color effect – yellow. We used the check to pay for electricity that we have already used, so all of the value has been consumed. Therefore, this is an expense. In our company, we lump these types of expenses in together and call them 'utilities'. Because we are increasing a green expense account, we use the same color effect – green."

Pops was beaming. "Do you get how well you understand this? Just think how far you have come in such a short time." He then added the $150 expense to our storyboard along with the appropriate green and yellow dotted lines connecting the amounts to green assets and yellow expenses in our storyboard.

12.6 **Z-Mart** effect of electricity expense

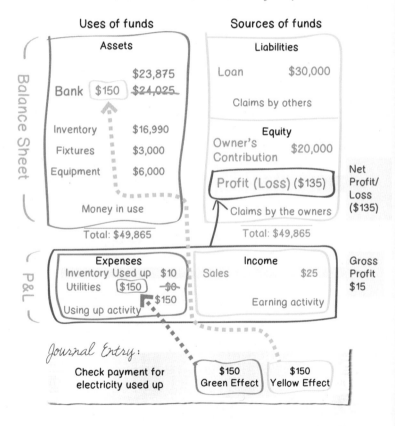

Pointing at the storyboard, he said, "Now this is starting to tell an interesting story. We can see that the gross profit on our sales is still $15, but we have another expense now of $150. If we prepare a mini profit-and-loss statement, it might look like this."

	Income	$25
Less	Cost of Sales	$10
Equals	Gross Profit	$15
Less	Other expenses	$150
Equals	Net Profit (loss)	($135)

He continued, "Now obviously we have only sold one cookbook so we made a gross profit of $15. My question is, how many of these cookbooks would we need to sell to cover the other expenses of $150 and thereby not operate at a loss?"

I looked back at my earlier diagram while I thought carefully about my answer.

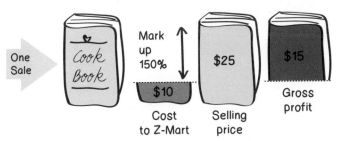

Break-even

I picked up a purple and green marker and illustrated my understanding of break-even: A series of 'cook-book gross profits' less the other expenses of $150 giving a net profit of $0.

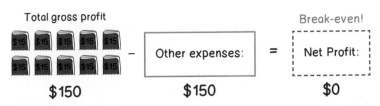

"If the sale of one cookbook contributes $15 gross profit, we would need to sell 10 cook books to cover the other expenses of $150 and break even. No profit and no loss," I concluded.

"Yes," he said emphatically.

"And," I said with a slight smile, "if our projected total of other expenses for the year was actually $300,000, then we would need to sell 20,000 cookbooks in a year to break even, 20,000 x $15 = $300,000. Lucky we sell more than just cookbooks."

"Double yes!" Pops agreed with a quick chuckle. "Calculating the break-even point is fairly straightforward with a few different ways we can do it. My final question to think about before our next meeting is how assets and expenses can be on the same side of the storyboard when they seem to be so different?"

"I'll be ready!" I retorted.

"Great. We'll also explore the notion that we don't always get the cash at the same time as we earn the income. Sometimes we allow people to pay us later, and sometimes we make them pay in advance. We'll take a look at expenses as well, sometimes we pay for the expenses in advance, and sometimes we pay for them later."

As I gathered up my colored pens and markers and closed my notebook, I thanked Pops for his help. "You know," I said, "I'm beginning to like accounting, it makes business come alive much more than I imagined."

"Fancy that," Pops said with a smile.

Yr1   Yr2   Yr3   Yr4

CHAPTER 13
TAKE CARE: PROFIT AND CASH DON'T ALWAYS PLAY NICELY TOGETHER

The next day at work, I thought about Pops' question regarding the difference between assets and expenses. What he had said made perfect sense in light of what I had learned, but my experience was telling me that assets and expenses were quite different so I questioned how both could be on the same side of the storyboard. Assets are surely good things to have, but expenses are considered bad. We're always being told to cut expenses at work.

I had another look at the storyboard to see what it could tell me. Then it came to me in a flash. Assets and expenses are on the same side of the storyboard because they are both uses of funds. Assets are funds 'in use', and expenses are funds 'used up'.

We acquire assets, usually by spending money, and those assets are valuable to the business. When we spend money on expenses, there is no real ongoing value – it's all used up or consumed. I had always thought that expenses are a necessary negative part of running a business because they don't provide an ongoing value to the organization in the way that assets do – their value has all been used up, expended, trashed, lost.

That evening, we reconvened and I explained the key difference between assets and expenses.

"Great!" Pops said with satisfaction. "Could you give me an actual example?"

"I thought you might ask that!" I began. "So the first example that came to mind was the new window you installed last year in the front of the shop. The cost of that new window might be seen as an expense to the business. But because it has value and will continue to add value for a number of years to come, it must be classified as an asset. However, you would classify the cleaning of the windows that JJ's Window Cleaning Service does each week as an expense. Of course, it's nice to have clean windows and the cleanliness supports the earning of income, but there's no enduring value to the business like there is with the actual window itself."

"Good explanation! So let's move on. Are you ready to learn one of the key aspects of business that most people just don't understand?" he asked with that twinkle in his eye.

"You bet! Bring it on, Sensei."

"If all goes well," Pops continued, "the business will make lots of sales and, hopefully, earn lots of profits. But even though we make a sale in one month and, therefore, increase our income and profit margins, our customers may not pay us the cash they owe us immediately. Depending on our policy for giving credit to our customers, that lag time between their purchase and their payment to us might be 30, 45, or even 90 days. So far, in our examples, our customers have paid us at the time of sale, and this is called a cash sale," Pops said. "Other times our customers may be required to pay us before the sale, which means Z-Mart would have the cash in the bank account before having earned it."

"At Z-Mart, don't most of our customers pay us in cash at the time of the sale?" I offered.

"That's right," he agreed as he filled out a new Z-Mart storyboard that captured all of our previous work. "But our policies also allow some families to have an open account with us so we make sales to these customers and collect the money the following month. Of course, we keep track of those credit sales so we know how much they owe us. We record it like this." He added a $200 credit sale in the new journal box he had just drawn and connected the amounts with a dotted line to a green receivables account under assets and a similar line to the yellow sales account under the income heading.

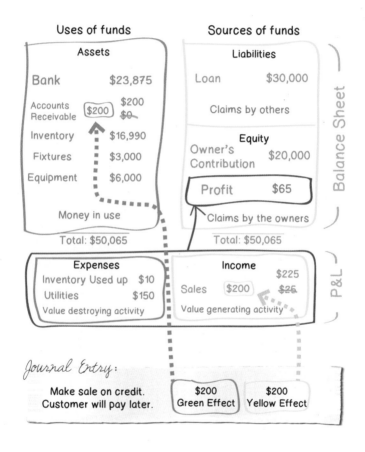

13.1 Z-Mart effects of credit sale

Uses of funds

Assets

Bank	$23,875
Accounts Receivable	$200 ($200) $0
Inventory	$16,990
Fixtures	$3,000
Equipment	$6,000

Money in use

Total: $50,065

Sources of funds

Liabilities

| Loan | $30,000 |

Claims by others

Equity

| Owner's Contribution | $20,000 |
| Profit | $65 |

Claims by the owners

Total: $50,065

Balance Sheet

Expenses

| Inventory Used up | $10 |
| Utilities | $150 |

Value destroying activity

Income

| | $225 |
| Sales | $200 $25 |

Value generating activity

P&L

Journal Entry:

Make sale on credit.
Customer will pay later.

$200 Green Effect $200 Yellow Effect

"So the business still records the sale, which increases income and profit even though it doesn't have the money yet?" I questioned. "But that doesn't seem right somehow."

"I assure you it's correct," he said. "The income is recorded when we earn the right to be paid. If we choose to allow the customer to pay later, that doesn't change the fact that we still earned the income in that month. It's quite normal for a business to try to gain extra sales by offering credit to their customers."

"Oh. But what if they don't pay, won't our income will be overstated?" I asked.

"Yes," Pops agreed, "the profit figures would be overstated, "But once we come to believe that they are not going to pay, we can effectively cancel out the original sale transaction then. We would reduce the value of the account receivable and that loss in asset value would be recorded as an expense, which we would call 'Bad debts'. As you know, only a small percentage of customers don't pay, and I'm afraid that's just the cost of offering credit terms."

"I see," I pondered, continuing my line of questioning, "But how is it that someone owing money to the business can be classified as an asset? It's not as good as cash, surely?"

"The receivable is like an IOU from the customer to the business, and it is valuable because it represents money that is yet to come into the bank account – a future cash inflow," Pops explained. "In fact, if you sold the business, you could sell these receivables to the next owner. Remember that we like being owed money. It's not quite as good as having cold, hard cash, but it's a good second best."

"I think I get it now," I said pointing to the last storyboard. "When the credit customer eventually pays, we record that event by increasing the bank account by the amount paid with a corresponding decrease to the amount owed to us, the receivable."

"Exactly," Pops concurred, "And the business must keep accurate tabs on its receivables and cash collections. You can imagine how important credit tracking is if all of your sales are on credit. Collecting the owed money would be a major activity of a credit-heavy business."

"OK, I get this now," I said, "But why would a customer pay in advance?"

"Many businesses operate this way," he said, "and I'm sure you've even been one of these customers. For example, when you buy tickets to events, memberships, subscriptions, insurance, and travel, you often pay in advance. At Z-Mart, our customers don't special order much but when they do we ask them to pay a deposit before we order what they want from our supplier. When this happens, we record the transaction like this." Pops quickly sketched out a new storyboard carrying over elements from the previous one. He gave the special order a value of $450 and drew appropriate lines from a new journal entry he created at the bottom of the storyboard. As he drew, he explained the green and yellow dotted lines and the placement of the $450 in the storyboard.

13.2 **Z-Mart** effects of prepayment

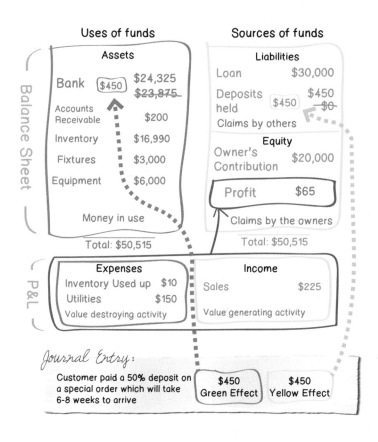

Uses of funds

Assets

Bank $450	$24,325 ~~$23,875~~
Accounts Receivable	$200
Inventory	$16,990
Fixtures	$3,000
Equipment	$6,000

Money in use

Total: $50,515

Sources of funds

Liabilities

Loan	$30,000
Deposits held $450	$450 ~~$0~~
Claims by others	

Equity

Owner's Contribution	$20,000
Profit	$65

Claims by the owners

Total: $50,515

Balance Sheet

Expenses

Inventory Used up	$10
Utilities	$150

Value destroying activity

Income

Sales	$225

Value generating activity

P&L

Journal Entry:

Customer paid a 50% deposit on a special order which will take 6-8 weeks to arrive

| $450 Green Effect | $450 Yellow Effect |

81

"You can see that the cash has been banked and we have recorded the fact that we still owe the customer for this order," he said. "In effect, we have made a promise, so we owe the associated goods or services to that customer. It's a liability. Once the order has arrived and we have earned the right to be paid, then we can say we have made the sale and we can record that event then."

"I get that," I said. "So, once we have earned the right to be paid, then we can decrease the 'Deposits held' liability to zero and show the sale amount in the income section because we've earned it."

"That's right," Pops confirmed. "And what do you think might be the advantage of being paid in advance like this?"

"Well, if it is an expensive order, the advance payment will ensure that they won't change their mind and stick us with return shipping costs on the special order item," I ventured. Encouraged by his nodding, I continued. "Also, if we have our normal credit terms with our suppliers, we won't have to pay for the order until 30 days after the supplier sells it to us. So we have the customer's money for 6 to 8 weeks plus 30 days. We could invest it!"

"It is a tremendous advantage for a business to be paid in advance for exactly the reasons you have given," he said. "Though of course they do have to keep track of the future sales amounts they are holding as IOUs in liabilities and ensure they deliver on their promise to the customers. I'm going to show you the three timing differences for income."

INCOME SCENARIO 1:
Cash received at the same time as income earned.

1

The most straightforward income scenario has us being paid at the same time as earning the income.

On the timeline below, Rosie the Riveter represents the earning happening in January, and the coin represents cash coming in as payment for the services in January.

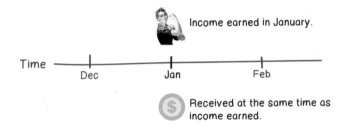

Income earned in January.

Time — Dec | Jan | Feb

Received at the same time as income earned.

On the *Color Accounting Framework* this is captured with two ↑ arrows showing more cash and more income.

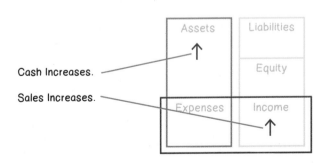

Cash Increases.

Sales Increases.

Assets	Liabilities
↑	Equity
Expenses	Income
	↑

INCOME SCENARIO 2:
Cash received first, income earned later.

2

Sometimes customers pay first and we earn the income later.

On the timeline below, the coin represents us receiving payment in December, marked with (a). Later, in January, we earn the income, represented again by Rosie, next to the (b).

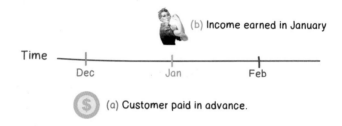

(b) **Income earned in January**

Time —————————————————
        Dec   Jan   Feb

(a) **Customer paid in advance.**

In December, the payment (a) is on the Framework below, causing assets (cash) to increase ↑ and the liabilities (services owed) to increase ↑ as well.

A month later, in January, the earning (b) on the Framework: Income (sales) increases ↑ and liabilities (services owed) decrease ↓.

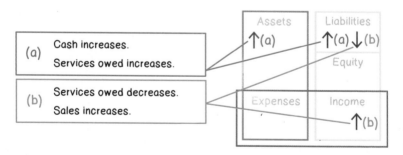

(a) Cash increases.
Services owed increases.

(b) Services owed decreases.
Sales increases.

Assets	Liabilities
↑(a)	↑(a) ↓(b)
	Equity
Expenses	Income
	↑(b)

Note how the end result of the two transaction is the same as where the cash transaction left us, with a 'detour' via the services owed liability: more income and more cash.

INCOME SCENARIO 3:
Earn income first, receive payment later.

3

Often we earn the income first and the customers pay us later.

On the timeline below, we first see Rosie earning the income in January, marked with (a). Later, in February, we see the coin representing the receipt of money for the services marked with (b).

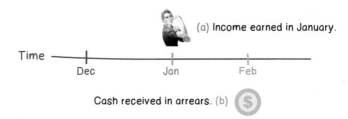

(a) **Income earned in January.**

Cash received in arrears. (b)

In January, the earning (a) on the Framework causes assets (accounts receivable) to increase ↑ and Income (sales) to increase ↑.

In February, the payment (b) on the Framework causes the asset (accounts receivable) to decrease ↓ and the other asset (cash) to increase ↑.

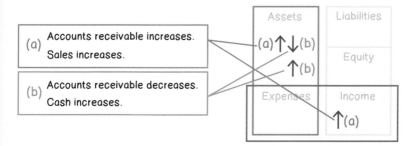

Again, note how in the end we are back to where the cash transaction left us, with a 'detour' via the accounts receivable asset.

I noticed a new term in his drawing and asked about the meaning. "What does 'in arrears' mean?"

"It means that the money changes hands after the event. In this example, we made a sale and earned income, but we didn't get paid until later because we gave the customer time to pay. Sometimes it can be called back payment or balance due."

"Let me see if I've got this," I said. "I need to compare when the cash changed hands to when Z-Mart earned the income in January – it's all about the timing of each aspect.

"The first scenario in our timeline diagram shows that we earned the income and received the cash for it in January. So the cash impact and profit effect will both happen in January.

"In the second scenario of our drawing timeline our business received cash into our bank account in December, but the profit effect doesn't hit the framework until January.

"In the third scenario, we earned the income in January so the profit effect is recorded in January. But we didn't get the cash until February so that impact on our bank account will be in the February balance sheet."

Pops, my Sensei, was pretty pleased with himself now. His student was really getting it.

"Pops, I feel good about what I've learned," I said, "but I was thinking about the timing difference between earning income and the cash coming in. I suppose the same concept applies to expenses, too. You have to manage both the profit effect and the impact on available cash."

EXPENSE SCENARIO 1:
Business pays at the same time of service.

The most straightforward expense scenario is when we pay at the same time as when we incur the expense.

On the timeline below, the light bulb represents the incurrence of the expense in January, and the coin represents cash going out in January to pay for the expense.

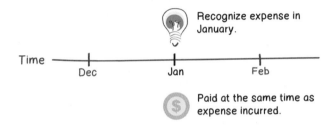

Recognize expense in January.

Time — Dec — Jan — Feb

Paid at the same time as expense incurred.

On the *Color Accounting Framework* this is shown with an increase ↑ arrow reflecting more expense and a decrease arrow ↓ showing less assets (cash).

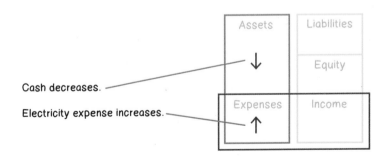

Cash decreases.

Electricity expense increases.

EXPENSE SCENARIO 2:
Business prepays for service.

2

Sometimes we pay first and we incur an expense later, for example when we use pre-paid electricity after paying for it.

On the timeline below, the coin represents us paying cash out in December, marked with (a). Later, in January, we incur the expense by using the electricity, shown by the light bulb with the (b).

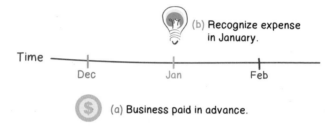

(b) Recognize expense in January.

(a) Business paid in advance.

On the Framework below, in December, the payment (a) is causing one asset (cash) to decrease ↓ and another asset (prepaid electricity expense) to increase ↑.

A month later, in January, the expense (b) is causing assets (prepaid electricity) to decrease ↓ and expenses (electricity expense) to increase ↑.

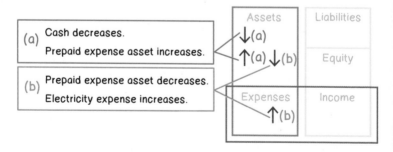

(a) Cash decreases.
Prepaid expense asset increases.

(b) Prepaid expense asset decreases.
Electricity expense increases.

Note how the end result of the two transaction is the same as the cash transaction, with a 'detour' via the prepaid expense asset: more expenses and less cash.

EXPENSES SCENARIO 3:
Business receives service, pays later.

3

Sometimes we incur an expense first and pay for it later, like when we use electricity and pay for it later.

On the timeline below, the light bulb, marked with (a), represents us incurring an expense in January. In February, we pay for the expense with cash, shown by the coin (b).

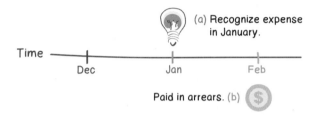

(a) **Recognize expense in January.**

Time — Dec — Jan — Feb

Paid in arrears. (b)

On the Framework below, in December the expense (a) is causing liabilities (accounts payable) to increase ↑ and expenses to increase ↑.

A month later, in January, the payment (b) is causing assets (cash) to decrease ↓ and liabilities (accounts payable) to also decrease ↓.

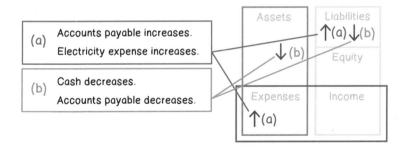

Note how the end result of the two transaction is the same as the cash transaction, with a 'detour' via the accounts payable liability: more expenses and less cash.

"You absolutely must manage your cash flows, in and out, if you want to stay in business, Craig," Pops said.

The drawings really helped me understand the concepts that Pops was describing.

Pops continued, "Sometimes businesses just focus on the profit effect and say, 'Oh look – we're making huge profits this year.' But if the business is not collecting the cash from their customers, they will run out of cash pretty quickly. I've seen companies run out of cash and die because of this mistake of only focusing on the income statement and not noticing what was happening with cash and accounts receivable on the balance sheet."

"On the other hand," he explained, "some people only look at the cash side and take on customer orders or make sales that are just not profitable. That's OK every now and then, but it's not a sustainable business model."

CHAPTER 14
CONTINUING TO LEARN

A week later Pops and I met for coffee at a local restaurant. I told him I was feeling confident I could start my business now.

"I'd say you are well prepared," Pops responded with a bit of pride about his student's success. "You already know more than many people, and what you have is a framework that allows you to continue to learn.

"You see, the model with the five boxes that we've called the *Color Accounting Framework,* or 'storyboard', is all-encompassing. Everything financial that happens in a business falls inside the framework and can be described using it. Of course, there are nuances and perhaps some jargon that you may not recognize at first when having financial conversations with colleagues. But I can tell you, anything you hear is just a variation on what you've learned. And I should point out, a lot of people - you'd be surprised how many - use jargon without an understanding of the fundamentals. You're in much better shape if you know the fundamentals and just need to ask the meaning of jargon. There's always more to learn about business and finances, and I encourage you to read and learn more," Pops counseled. "Combined with passion, determination, and vision, you will accomplish a great deal. Like Dr Seuss says, 'Oh! The places you'll go!'"

I nodded to myself, sensing that his prediction was spot on.

The Color Accounting Parable

PART 2 FINANCIAL ANALYSIS

Amazing things happen
when you let go.

Amazing things happen when you let go. Three years ago, when I finally sat down with my grandfather to learn about accounting and the fundamentals of business, I never imagined how my life would take an exciting turn. What a rewarding journey of ongoing learning and discovery it has been since then.

I did set up my own business – a retail store called Freedom Retail - not far from Z-Mart, and, I'm proud to say, it's going quite well. Financially, it's not where I would like it to be, but it's profitable and sales are growing.

That said, I've made a few mistakes. Though I hate to admit it, it's been a great learning experience. I'll tell you more about the mistakes in a moment.

First, let me show you the balance sheet and income statement that are essential to managing my business.

As you know, the balance sheet tells you the financial position of the business; what assets the business has, and how it funded those assets through debt, stockholder's contributions to equity, and profits left in the business for growth. The Income Statement describes the financial performance of the business; how it is generating and sacrificing value through its operations, with the intention of growing its equity by generating more value than it is sacrificing.

Previously, when I looked at a set of financial statements I was overwhelmed by what occurred, for me, as a blur of stripes. I didn't know where to begin making sense of it and it didn't tell me a meaningful story.

Freedom Retail, Inc
Balance Sheet at December 31st 2018

	2018	2017
ASSETS		
Current Assets		
Cash and Deposits	46,083	291,383
Accounts Receivable	132,178	24,763
Inventories	238,885	97,517
Total Current Assets	417,146	413,663
ASSETS		
Non-Current Assets		
Land & Buildings	502,425	456,000
Equipment, fixtures & fittings	176,273	83,973
Investment in other companies	1,584	1,584
Total Non-Current Assets	680,282	541,557
TOTAL ASSETS	1,097,428	955,220
LIABILITIES		
Current Liabilities		
Borrowings	63,566	34,360
Payables	182,475	62,130
Provisions	31,143	16,048
Total Current Liabilities	277,184	112,538
Non-Current Liabilities		
Borrowings	548,765	612,331
Total Non-Current Liabilities	548,765	612,331
TOTAL LIABILITIES	825,949	724,869
EQUITY		
Issued Capital: 192,160 shares	192,160	192,160
Retained profits	79,319	38,191
TOTAL EQUITY	271,479	230,351

Freedom Retail, Inc
Income Statement for the year ending 2018

	2018	2017
SALES	**1,456,560**	**904,928**
LESS: COST OF SALES EXPENSES		
Purchases - Products Used	857,545	547,301
Sales commissions	79,443	0
	936,988	547,301
GROSS PROFIT	519,572	357,627
LESS: OTHER EXPENSES		
Accounting and book-keeping	8,256	6,330
Advertising	25,858	1,664
Bad debts expense	6,358	832
Bank charges	4,951	2,785
Depreciation	29,282	18,656
Employment expenses	207,429	120,548
Insurance	28,047	24,520
Interest paid	15,089	11,733
Rental of office equipment	1,756	0
Shop rental	103,574	96,473
Sponsorships	2,611	2,022
Telephone & Utilities	8,835	7,307
Other	17,920	15,954
	459,966	308,824
PROFIT - before tax	**59,606**	**48,803**
Less: Income Tax Expense	18,478	15,129
PROFIT - after tax	**41,128**	**33,674**
Add: retained profits at start of year	38,191	4,517
RETAINED PROFIT at end of year	79,319	38,191

Now, when I look at the balance sheet of my business, I know that to make sense of it I must keep in mind the principles that Pops taught me. In particular, I remember the meaning of the three main parts of the balance sheet by recalling the definitions of the terms; assets, liabilities, and equity.

Looking at the balance sheet, this is what I keep in mind for each section:

Assets

Valuable Things
These are the valuable things that the business owns or controls. Their primary purpose is to generate income and profit, either directly or indirectly. We are trying to grow them.

Liabilities

Claims of 'Outsiders'
This is the intangible funding from outsiders to buy the assets. They have first claim on the assets.

Equity

Claims of Owners
This is the intangible funding by the owner to buy the assets. Some equity is contributed and the rest is earned as profits and retained in the business.

Freedom Retail, Inc
Balance Sheet at December 31st 2018

	2018	2017
ASSETS		
Current Assets		
Cash and Deposits	46,083	291,383
Accounts Receivable	132,178	24,763
Inventories	238,885	97,517
Total Current Assets	417,146	413,663
ASSETS		
Non-Current Assets		
Land & Buildings	502,425	456,000
Equipment, fixtures & fittings	176,273	83,973
Investment in other companies	1,584	1,584
Total Non-Current Assets	680,282	541,557
TOTAL ASSETS	1,097,428	955,220
LIABILITIES		
Current Liabilities		
Borrowings	63,566	34,360
Payables	182,475	62,130
Provisions	31,143	16,048
Total Current Liabilities	277,184	112,538
Non-Current Liabilities		
Borrowings	548,765	612,331
Total Non-Current Liabilities	548,765	612,331
TOTAL LIABILITIES	825,949	724,869
EQUITY		
Issued Capital: 192,160 shares	192,160	192,160
Retained profits	79,319	38,191
TOTAL EQUITY	271,479	230,351

When looking at the Income Statement, I keep in mind the meanings of the sections as I'm reading through them:

Income	**Value generation** This is the value that the business has generated through its operations.
Direct Cost of Sales Expenses	**Direct value sacrifice to make sales** This is the sacrifice that the business made in order to directly generate each sale. These sacrifices grow in proportion to the sales growth.
Gross Profit	**Net sales value generated** This is the net value generated through sales. This profit can be used to run the business, pay taxes, reward stockholders, repay debt and grow the assets.
Overheads/ Indirect Expenses	**More value sacrifice to run business** This is the value destroyed in order to run the business itself after the Cost of the Sales has been incurred.
Net Profit Before Tax	**Another net value calculation** This is the net value generated after taking into account the expenses of running the business.
Tax Expense	**Final value sacrifice to pay taxes** Calculated on the net profit, this is a compulsory value sacrifice imposed by the government.
Net Profit After Tax	**Final net value generated figure** This is the net value generated after all expenses and taxes have been deducted. Used to reward owners, repay debt and invest in assets.

Freedom Retail, Inc
Income Statement for the year ending 2018

	2018	2017
SALES	**1,456,560**	**904,928**
LESS: COST OF SALES EXPENSES		
Purchases - Products Used	857,545	547,301
Sales commissions	79,443	0
	936,988	547,301
GROSS PROFIT	519,572	357,627
LESS: OTHER EXPENSES		
Accounting and book-keeping	8,256	6,330
Advertising	25,858	1,664
Bad debts expense	6,358	832
Bank charges	4,951	2,785
Depreciation	29,282	18,656
Employment expenses	207,429	120,548
Insurance	28,047	24,520
Interest paid	15,089	11,733
Rental of office equipment	1,756	0
Shop rental	103,574	96,473
Sponsorships	2,611	2,022
Telephone & Utilities	8,835	7,307
Other	17,920	15,954
	459,966	308,824
PROFIT - before tax	**59,606**	**48,803**
Less: Income Tax Expense	18,478	15,129
PROFIT - after tax	**41,128**	**33,674**
Add: retained profits at start of year	38,191	4,517
RETAINED PROFIT at end of year	79,319	38,191

If Pops were drawing up the 2018 accounts in his five-box *Color Accounting Framework*, which integrates the balance sheet and income statement, he would have drawn something like this:

USES OF FUNDS

SOURCES OF FUNDS

Balance Sheet

ASSETS	
Current Assets	
Cash and Deposits	46,083
Accounts Receivables	132,178
Inventories	238,885
Total Current Assets	**417,146**
ASSETS	
Non-Current Assets	
Land & Buildings	502,425
Equipment, fixtures & fittings	176,273
Investment in other companies	1,584
Total Non-Current Assets	**680,282**
TOTAL ASSETS	1,097,428

LIABILITIES	
Current Liabilities	
Borrowings	63,566
Payables	182,475
Provisions	31,143
Total Current Liabilities	**277,184**
Non-Current Liabilities	
Borrowings	548,765
Total Non-Current Liabilities	**548,765**
TOTAL LIABILITIES	825,949

EQUITY	
Issued Capital: 192,160 shares	192,160
Retained profits	79,319
TOTAL EQUITY	271,479

Profit 41,128

Income Statement

COST OF SALES EXPENSES	
Purchases - Products Used	857,545
Sales commissions	79,443
	936,988
OTHER EXPENSES	
Accounting and book-keeping	8,256
Advertising	25,858
Bad debts expense	6,358
Bank charges	4,951
Depreciation	29,282
Employment expenses	207,429
Insurance	28,047
Interest paid	15,089
Rental of office equipment	1,756
Shop rental	103,574
Sponsorships	2,611
Telephone & Utilities	8,835
Other	17,920
	459,966
Income Tax Expense	18,478
TOTAL EXPENSES	1,415,432

How we calculate the Retained Profits:

> 2017 Closing Retained Profits
> **38,191**
>
> **+** Profit **41,128**
>
> **=** 2018 Closing Retained Profits
> **79,319**

SALES 1,456,560

Reading the balance sheet and income statement together, I've learned that the essence of the business story they tell reads something like this:

A ASSETS

On December 31st 2018, Freedom Retail had assets totaling **$1,097,428** in use *for the purpose of generating a return for the owner.*

L LIABILITIES

Freedom partially funded those assets with **$825,949** of debt, which equates to 75% of the total asset value.

E EQUITY

The remaining portion (25%) of the assets in the amount of **$271,479** was funded by Freedom's one shareholder (**me**).

INCOME

In 2018, Freedom *generated value for its shareholder* by earning **$1,456,560** in sales revenue.

EXPENSES

In order to deliver those sales, Freedom sacrificed **$1,415,432** of value (= $936,988 directly + $459,966 indirectly, and $18,478) as expenses and taxes...

NET PROFIT

...resulting in a net profit after tax of **$41,128**, which is included in the equity number (shareholder's funds) above.

Now that I'm familiar and comfortable with the layout of the financial statements, I'm getting more skilled at noticing the numbers themselves. Pops is encouraging me to further develop these financial analysis skills. Financial analysis is like wearing a different hat compared with bookkeeping. Bookkeeping is storytelling. Whereas financial analysis is interpreting the story and deciding whether it's good, bad, or otherwise; it is an exercise in judgment. Bookkeeping is telling, financial analysis is interpreting.

Wearing my financial analysis hat, I notice the significant changes of the numbers.

I've learned to compare two or more time periods to each other to see how the various accounts, like cash, accounts receivable, inventory, and accounts payable have changed between the periods.

ANALYZING THE INCOME STATEMENT

Let me show you what happened on the Income Statement.

Sales

As you can see, sales grew from $904,928 in 2017 to $1,456,560 in 2018. That's an increase of $551,632, or in percentage terms, an increase of 61%. All other considerations aside, this is a good thing. Many businesses would be thrilled to see their sales grow by 61% in a year. Judging by sales alone, you could say that Freedom Retail is 'on a tear'.

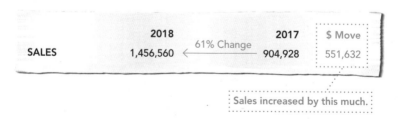

	2018		2017	$ Move
SALES	1,456,560	← 61% Change	904,928	551,632

Sales increased by this much.

However, the story is not quite as simple as that…

Cost of Sales (direct expenses)

To grow the sales we hired some new sales staff on a commission basis.

LESS: COST OF SALES EXPENSE	2018		2017	$ Move
		57% Change		
Purchases - Products Used	857,545 ←		547,301	310,244
Sales Commissions	79,443	71% Change	0	79,443
	936,988 ←		547,301	389,687

The commissions we paid the sales staff are considered a direct expense. This is because they are directly linked to each sale. Every time there's a sale, there's a commission expense. Therefore they are counted as a Cost of Sales. The commissions expense which wasn't there in 2017 but appeared in 2018 made our Total Cost of Sale increase from 60% to 64% of sales.

	2018	% of Sale	2017	% of Sale
Purchases - Products Used	1,456,560 ←		904,928 ←	
LESS: COST OF SALES EXPENSE				
Purchases - Products Used	857,545		547,301	
Sales Commissions	79,443		0	
	936,988	64%	547,301	60%

In other words, it's costing us more to make each sale, BUT, we are making a lot more sales. If the math works, that's okay. Even though we give away a little more of the pie every time we make a sale, we end up with more pie in total. Let's see how.

> Cost of Sale increased by 4% points.

Gross Profit

Gross profit is the difference between sales and the cost of sales. The gross profit margin is gross profit expressed as a percentage of the total sales figure.

	2018	% of Sale	2017	% of Sale
SALES	1,456,560 ←		904,928 ←	
less Cost of Sales Expense not shown, gives gross profit …				
GROSS PROFIT	519,572	36%	357,627	40%

In 2018 the gross profit margin was $519,572 ÷ $1,456,560 x 100, which is 36%. The previous year the 'GPM' was 40%.

Freedom Retail's gross profit margin decreased by 4% points because the Cost of Sales percentage increased – they are inversely related.

When the cost of sales percentage was 60% the gross profit margin was 40%.

And in 2018 when the cost of sales percentage went up to 64% the gross profit margin went down to 36%.

Clearly, you can see how the gross profit margin plus the cost of sales percent make 100% (of sales).

As you can see in the extract on the next page, the cost of sale account "Purchases - Products used" (inventory used up) dropped a little as a percentage of sales. It went from 60% to 59%.

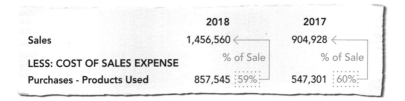

	2018		2017	
Sales	1,456,560		904,928	
LESS: COST OF SALES EXPENSE		% of Sale		% of Sale
Purchases - Products Used	857,545	59%	547,301	60%

This was partly because we were able to raise our prices a little bit as our reputation for great service began to spread. This year it should improve a bit more, as we negotiate better pricing from our suppliers because we are buying more and are paying them consistently.

Note: Remember that 'inventory consumed' (expense) is not the same as 'inventory' bought (asset). When we buy inventory, it is recorded as an asset. When we sell that inventory, each sale generates a cost of sale for the inventory that was consumed in that sale and a corresponding reduction in the asset value of inventory.

Net Profit After Tax

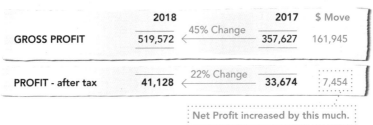

	2018		2017	$ Move
GROSS PROFIT	519,572	45% Change	357,627	161,945
PROFIT - after tax	41,128	22% Change	33,674	7,454

Net Profit increased by this much.

Even though the store made $161,945 more gross profit in 2018 than 2017 (the difference between $519,572 and $357,627), at the end of the year after all expenses and taxes were paid the store only made $7,454 more net profit.

Profit increased in one year from $33,674 to $41,128. That was rather disappointing, given that we increased sales by over half a million dollars. So what happened?

Indirect Expenses

The reason the net profit after tax increased by so little compared with sales or gross profit is because the indirect expenses also increased quite a bit, $151,142 to be precise.

	2018	49% Change	2017	$ Move
Total indirect expenses	**459,966**	←	**308,824**	151,142

Indirect, or 'Overhead' expenses are sacrifices the business makes that aren't linked directly to each sale, but which are incurred to keep the business running. Rent and electricity are typical examples of overhead expenses in a retail environment. Whether or not sales happen, rent has to be paid.

In 2018 all the indirect expense accounts increased. But as an ambitious business owner, I chose to increase some indirect expenses significantly.

The main ones that increased were:

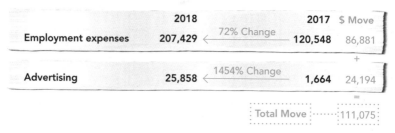

	2018		2017	$ Move
Employment expenses	**207,429**	72% Change ←	**120,548**	86,881
				+
Advertising	**25,858**	1454% Change ←	**1,664**	24,194
			=	
		Total Move		111,075

Just those two categories accounted for $111,075 of extra expenses.

In retrospect, I might have overdone the staffing and advertising. But while it was disappointing to only make an extra $7,454 net profit after tax on an increase in sales of over $551,632, I'm confident that we will see big benefits next year. Sales should continue to climb, but we won't have to incur another increase in base salary expenses for some time. Consequently, our net profit after tax should increase substantially.

Forecasting

Forecasting, as the name implies, is about looking into the future to guess how the numbers could change.

For example, if I hold the advertising to the same level and we manage to increase sales by about 20% in 2019 (that is, an increase of $300,000 = 20% of $1,456,560), this will give us an extra $108,000 of gross profit assuming our gross profit margin remains at 36% of sales (36% of approximately $300,000 = $108,000). And if we manage to hold all the other indirect expenses the same, then this $108,000 would flow through to the 'bottom line', causing an increase in net profit of $108,000 too. Of course our tax would increase, so while net profit before tax will benefit fully, the increase in net profit after tax will be proportionately less.

ANALYZING THE BALANCE SHEET

Okay, I'm stalling here… a bit embarrassed to tell you about my mistakes.

We've been focusing above on the Profit & Loss Statement, also known as the Income Statement. That's the report that tells us how the business has performed. It's like the video camera that describes the activities of the business during each period. It's a 'verb-statement'. And you've got a sense that as an ambitious new business owner, I pushed hard to grow the business. Indeed I succeeded, as sales grew by over 60%. That's quite an impressive result, taken by itself. I would say that the big factors in the business' growth were the introduction of the commission structure for the sales staff and the increased expenditure on advertising, as well as our commitment to client service.

Everything looks good right? Wrong.

With some coaching from Pops I realized that I'd focused too much on chasing sales growth. More specifically, while I was pushing the business hard to grow sales, I took my eye off the balance sheet and didn't manage the various assets and liabilities as well as I could have.

I messed up the management of the balance sheet and that can be fatal.

Even as our sales went up by nearly two thirds, and we were still making some absolute profit gains, our cash in the bank at the end of 2018 had plummeted. In one year, it had dropped from $291,383 to $46,083.

Balance Sheet		
ASSETS	2018	2017
Short-term Assets	Big drop!	
Cash and short-term deposits	46,083 ⟵———	291,383

Ouch!

Sales is not cash

As they say, you can run a business without profits for a while, but you can't survive without cash. You must be able to pay your bills when they come due or it's all over. So, where did all that cash go?

I'd like to say that having only $46,000 cash in the bank was an overnight aberration, that the balance at December 31st was exceptionally low. After all, cash is a volatile, short-term balance sheet account. It goes up and down all the time as cash comes in and goes out. But the truth is that when I look back at the records, our average weekly bank balance had been steadily declining for a good part of 2018.

I have to admit, I got quite a fright. I had fallen into the trap of thinking that rising sales must be associated with rising levels of cash. How wrong

I was! Of course I called Pops to clear things up. And his answer was quite simple. Thankfully it wasn't too late.

Let me show you…

Cash

Cash, we've established, dropped by $245,300 in one year.

	2018		2017
		Dropped by 245,300	
Cash and short-term deposits	46,083	←	291,383

So where did it go? It went to a number of places.

Accounts Receivable

Part of my strategy to increase sales of Freedom Retail was to be more generous in allowing customers to pay us later. In the industry jargon, I loosened our credit terms to make more sales. We let more customers buy more from us on credit, and pay later. The benefit of doing this is that a business will make sales that it otherwise would not have made. The argument is that these customers would have gone elsewhere if we insisted that they pay cash at the time of the sale. The downside for us is that giving credit to customers delays the flow of cash into the business, and worse some customers may never pay, resulting in a bad debt expense. (Take note of that expense line in the Income Statement.)

Don't be too generous with accounts receivable

Freedom Retail's accounts receivable increased between year-ends by over $107,000, from $24,763 to $132,178. That is to say, Freedom had made sales to customers worth $132,178 that on December 31st hadn't yet been paid for. The customers owed Freedom $132,178 at year-end.

	2018		2017	Move $
Accounts Receivable	132,178	434% Change	24,763	107,415

As you know, when a customer buys from the store, the sale still shows up on the Income Statement even if the customer will pay for their purchases later. What the business has earned at the time of the sale instead of cash is the valuable right to receive cash, also known as an Account Receivable. Being owed money is still an asset, even if it isn't quite as desirable as cash itself.

But while customers are walking out with their goods 'on credit', the sales staff still need to be paid, the lights need to be kept running, and the inventory needs to be replenished. So cash continues to flow out of the business. Therefore an increase in accounts receivable can have a very dangerous downward impact on our available cash balance unless we manage the situation carefully.

By focusing too much on achieving sales we also lost sight of the aging of the accounts receivable. We were so busy with other things, we didn't stay on top of who owed us money and how long they were taking to pay.

So letting the business' accounts receivable increase so much was our first balance sheet mistake.

Don't tie-up too much cash in inventory

Inventory
Perhaps even worse than letting the accounts receivable account get out of control, I tied up too much of our cash in inventory.

The inventory balance on December 31st 2018 was $141, 368 more than last year.

	2018		2017	Move $
Inventories	238,885	145% Change	97,517	141,368

Of course the balances shown are two snapshots of the balance throughout the year. Just because the balance on December 31st was $238,885 it doesn't have to mean that the balance for the rest of the year was that high. The balance moves up or down everyday. But when I looked back at the monthly trend of the inventories balance, the average inventory balance did rise steadily throughout the year.

What makes my inventory mistake worse than my accounts receivable mistake is the fact that inventory is completely under one's own control. You can't always control when a customer is going to pay you, but I was entirely responsible for ordering the inventory.

I now know that tying up so much cash in inventory can be a terrible drain on our cash balances. Rather than tie up cash in inventory on the shelves, that cash could have been in the bank account and available to pay for other things instead.

Just-in-time inventory management is the practice of keeping inventory levels low and ordering the inventory required to make a sale just in time for that sale. Instead of a few big orders, the business makes lots of small orders – why buy it until you need it? While this means having less cash tied up in inventory, it can also result in higher inventory prices and an increase in delivery expenses. But that may be a small price to pay compared with running out of cash, or the nasty expense of borrowing money at the last minute to prop up the business. Looking back on it, perhaps my inventory management technique could be called 'Just-in-case' as I seemed to have every conceivable inventory item on the shelf, even if they weren't yet in season.

Establishing the appropriate inventory level is a fine art. If you have too much inventory, then you have too much cash tied up in the inventory. Furthermore, some of that inventory might expire or become obsolete. Old inventory may need to be discounted heavily to make it attractive for sale, or worse, thrown out and written off as an inventory write-down expense. Written-off means the amount of the asset value lost is moved to the expense account (without any offsetting sales income). And that hurts your profit margins.

But if your inventory level is too low, then you might run out of stock. And that's really bad because that means no sales until you restock. I once went into a fried chicken joint and they told me they'd run out of… guess what? Yes, chicken.

When the volcano in Iceland grounded most of the planes in Europe, and the tsunami in Japan damaged roads, a lot of car factories which used *just-in-time* inventory management had to close their doors temporarily. They ran out of parts to manufacture the cars. Missing even a small part like a door handle can hold up completion of a whole car. Since then, the car companies have been keeping more inventory on hand.

I'm realizing that running a business is quite an art. Sure I've made mistakes, but it's fun. It's like a machine with many different parts that need to be tuned and kept working.

Fixed Assets
As I stated earlier, I'm an ambitious and enthusiastic business owner.

My ambitions led me to buy some new Long-term Assets also known as 'Non-current Assets'. Non-current or Long-term means we expect them to last for more than 12 months.

The business built an extra storage room onto the back of the store and bought new display cabinets and equipment so we could make more sales. This is why the 'Total Long-term Assets' (shown below) went up from $541,557 to $680,282.

	2018		2017	Move $
Non-Current Assets				
Land & Buildings	502,425		456,000	46,425
Equipment, fixtures & fittings	176,273		83,973	92,300
Investment in other companies	1,584		1,584	0
Total Non-Current Assets	680,282 ←	Increase!	541,557	138,725

The assets shown in the balance sheet are shown at 'written down' or 'net book value'. Net book value is usually cost minus accumulated depreciation.

The table on the next page shows how Freedom started 2018 with non-current assets that had cost $575,798 and had been written down by $34,241 to give an opening net book value of $541,557.

Freedom then purchased another $168,007 of assets for a total of assets-at-cost of $743,805. This balance is reduced by the accumulated depreciation to show the net book value. The accumulated depreciation comprises the $34,241 brought forward from the 2017 year, as well as the additional depreciation expense of $29,282 from the 2018 year. This gives the final net book value of $680,282.

We ended with assets worth this much.

Throughout the year, we bought assets costing this much.

We started the year with equipment costing this much.

2018

Dec 31st ←——————— Jan 1st

	Closing	Movement	Opening
Cost	743,805	168,007	575,798
Accumulated Depreciation	(63,523)	(29,282)	(34,241)
Net Book Value	680,282	138,725	541,557

During the year, all the fixed assets lost this much on the books value, as you can see from the income statement.

Before this year, they had lost this much value.

You can see the $29,282 depreciation charge in the 2018 income statement:

	2018	2017
Depreciation	29,282	18,656

How I should've funded fixed assets

The mistake I made wasn't buying the assets. They've actually all been productive and helped us make more sales. The mistake was how the business funded them. We should have borrowed money to pay for them, leaving our precious cash in the bank for other things. Specifically, we should have taken out long-term loans to fund the long-term assets. There is a general rule of thumb that says the longevity of the asset should match the longevity of the loan.

But as you can see, instead of our long-term liabilities going up, they actually came down, from about $612,331 thousand to about $548,765 thousand.

If you look closely, you'll notice that what happened was a $63,566 portion of the Non-current loan became current. So it is now shown under Current Liabilities. And the 2017 current borrowing of $34,360 has been paid off.

Current Liabilities	2018	2017	Move $
Borrowings	63,566	34,360	29,206

Non-Current Liabilities	2018	2017	
Borrowings	548,765	612,331	(63,566)

Accounts Payable

The last glitch that I have to fess up to is our accounts payable, or creditors.

As you can see, at the end of 2018 we owed our suppliers $182,475 compared with $62,130 a year earlier.

	2018		2017
		Big increase!	
Payables	182,475	⟵	62,130

Don't abuse the payables

Paying creditors late and building up the accounts payable debt is a source of funding and will have a positive impact on our cash flows. But it is a short-term tactic that's not to be abused.

I quickly learned that we were paying our suppliers on average about 60 days after they supplied us, even though we'd agreed to pay them within 30 days. I'm now ashamed of that, and I realize that as my trusted business partners, I need to do the right thing by them. Not to mention save myself some late payment penalties. Some of the suppliers almost stopped supplying us with goods, which would've been disastrous. It was only when I personally called and promised that we were getting our cash flow under control that they agreed to continue to 'extend credit'.

An Auspicious Future

As you can see, there have been lots of lessons learned along the way. Fortunately none of them have been fatal to the business.

Every Friday morning, I'm now getting reports from my bookkeeper on the:

- Bank reconciliations
- Cash balances with projections
- Balance sheet
- Income Statement
- Accounts payable and receivable aging reports

As Pops told me, if I don't have regular reports on where the business stands and how it's performing, I'm 'flying blind'. He says that the biggest difference between successful and unsuccessful business owners is being on top of the numbers (and not just those in the Income Statement, but all the numbers).

And I believe him.

I'm planting myself firmly in the driving-with-clear-vision camp, running the business by the numbers and seeing a bright future for Freedom Retail.

APPENDIX
DEBITS AND CREDITS REVEALED

In *Color Accounting* we use the colors green and yellow in place of the jargon words 'debit' and 'credit'.

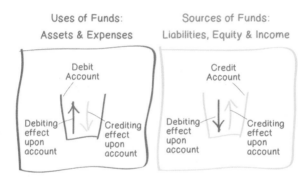

Uses of Funds: Assets & Expenses

Sources of Funds: Liabilities, Equity & Income

In traditional accounting language:

Green is debit
Yellow is credit

THE UNIVERSAL RULE

↑ To increase an account, use the same word (debit/debit or credit/credit)

↓ To decrease an account, use the opposite word (debit/credit or credit/debit)

An example: the Cash in Bank account (like the green bucket in the diagram on the previous page) is an asset to the business and therefore a debit-type account (green side).

Debiting **the bank account increases** it.

Crediting **the bank account decreases** it.

Note: When you receive a bank statement in the mail from your bank, money you have deposited shows up as a credit. That appears to be the opposite of what we're saying above. But the bank statement is from the perspective of the bank. It's their statement, not yours. The statement is a printout of the bank's liability to you. By receiving your deposit the bank owes you more money. Liability accounts are credit accounts, which is why a crediting effect increases the account. The bank is crediting their credit account. In your own accounting records, you would be debiting your matching debit account (as shown as in the diagram above).

And it is this very thing that tends to cause confusion for people trying to understand how debits and credits work in business. And it is also the reason why *Color Accounting* was invented in the first place.

AUTHORS:

Peter Frampton and Mark Robilliard are both Fellows of the Institute of Chartered Accountants in Australia and worked together at a "Big Four" accounting firm. Years after they struggled with the way accounting was taught at university, they decided that learning accounting didn't have to be an unpleasant and difficult experience. In 1992, they declared they would find a better way. This commitment led them to invent *Color Accounting*™, a visual way of representing financial information, teaching accounting, and explaining how business works.

Peter currently lives in the District of Columbia, United States and Mark in Queensland, Australia.

COLOR ACCOUNTING:

Color Accounting is identifiable by its colorful zebra mascot.

The *Color Accounting* system, patented in 2010, is licensed by Accounting Comes Alive International to independent sales and training partners in a growing list of countries including the USA, Canada, UK, Australia, South Korea, Japan, and South Africa.

In the United States, the *Color Accounting*® system is used at innovative universities such as Georgetown University, the University of Pennsylvania's

Wharton School of Executive Education, and American University. It is used by Wall Street banks, life insurance companies, law firms, government agencies, and many not-for-profit organizations.

If you like this book and its approach to business and accounting, you can find more at www.ColorAccounting.com.

PUBLISHER:

ACCOUNTING™
comes
ALIVE

Accounting Comes Alive International is the education and publishing company that owns, licenses, and trains the *Color Accounting* system .

Set yourself free